the arthuric·   ɔt

THE
ARTHURIAN
TAROT
—A HALLOWQUEST HANDBOOK—

caitlín and john matthews

THE AQUARIAN PRESS

First published 1990

British Library Cataloguing in Publication Data

Matthews, Caitlín
The Arthurian tarot: a hallowquest handbook.
1. Tarot cards
I. Title   II. Matthews, John
133.3'2424

ISBN 0-85030-755-4

The Aquarian Press is part of the Thorsons Publishing Group, Wellingborough, Northamptonshire, NN8 2RQ, England

Typeset by Harper Phototypesetters Limited, Northampton
Printed in Great Britain by Woolnoughs Bookbinding
Limited, Irthlingborough, Northamptonshire

1 3 5 7 9 10 8 6 4 2

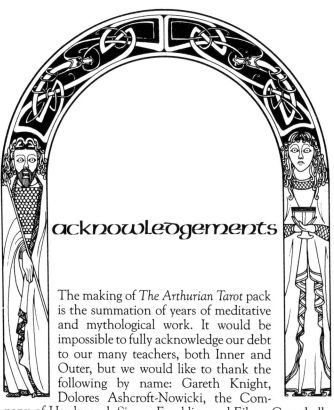

acknowledgements

The making of *The Arthurian Tarot* pack
is the summation of years of meditative
and mythological work. It would be
impossible to fully acknowledge our debt
to our many teachers, both Inner and
Outer, but we would like to thank the
following by name: Gareth Knight,
Dolores Ashcroft-Nowicki, the Com-
pany of Hawkwood, Simon Franklin, and Eileen Campbell.

The sample readings which appear in Chapter 4 were all
interpreted and selected by Caitlín from a number of clients
who consulted her in the early months of 1988. Our thanks to
everyone who helped us test-run the prototype *Hallowquest*
deck which at this stage still had to be redrafted by Miranda:
they permitted us to make use of their readings willingly, but
their names have of course been changed, as have certain
details.

Lastly, to Miranda Gray, our heartfelt gratitude for
conveying our vision in pictorial form so clearly.

To the Company of the Hallows

'if skill be of work or of will
in the dispersed homes of the household, let the Company
pray for it still.'

— *Charles Williams*, Taliesin Through Logres

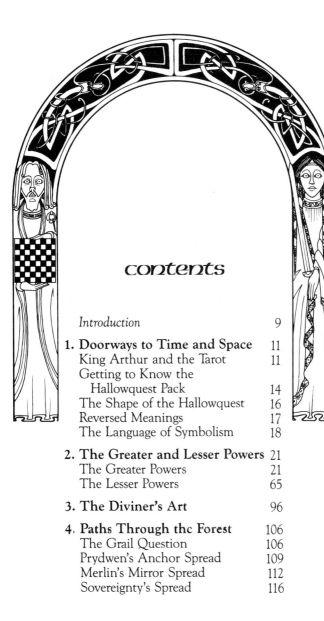

contents

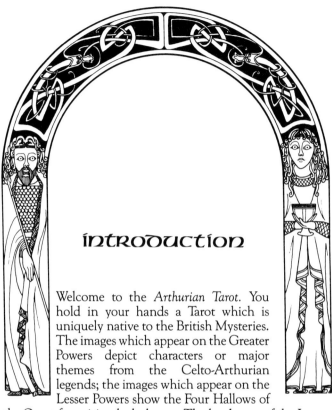

íntroductíon

Welcome to the *Arthurian Tarot*. You hold in your hands a Tarot which is uniquely native to the British Mysteries. The images which appear on the Greater Powers depict characters or major themes from the Celto-Arthurian legends; the images which appear on the Lesser Powers show the Four Hallows of the Quest for spiritual wholeness. The landscape of the Lesser Powers depicts the land of Britain itself. On the back of each card is depicted the Goddess of Sovereignty — the Goddess of the Land herself — with the empowering objects of the Quest: the Sword, Spear, Grail and Stone.

The Grail Quest is of course one which transcends national barriers and cultural divides. Spiritual wholeness is the natural goal of all people wherever they derive their heritage. However, our own imbalances set up a discordance between ourselves and the land. If we start working on finding personal spiritual wholeness, it soon becomes clear that our environment, our land and the whole planet are intimately associated with our own harmony. The native peoples of the world knew this and some still teach it. For many of us, particularly those who attempt to follow the native traditions of Britain, that teaching is obscure to us. It is for this reason that we go for wisdom and nourishment to the guiding myths of our own land — the Arthurian legends. The powerful archetypes underlying this tradition still have deep wisdom which will both instruct and encourage us if we seek their help.

This small handbook is designed to accompany the *Arthurian Tarot* deck and give support and a brief background to all seeking to use it for divinatory purposes. For those who wish to leave the beaten track and explore the hinterland of the British Mysteries and work with the Arthurian legends in a more magical way, there is an companion volume entitled *Hallowquest: Tarot Magic and the Arthurian Mysteries.* This gives meditations, shamanic journeys, rituals and teachings on the Mysteries which will lead you deeper into the native heritage of these islands.

The earth on which we walk is our mother and teacher, assuming many different faces depending on our inner condition. The wisdom of the earth is at last being heard after centuries of neglect. Whatever your native tradition, may you find your own Goddess of the Land and seek to wield her gifts with joy and courage!

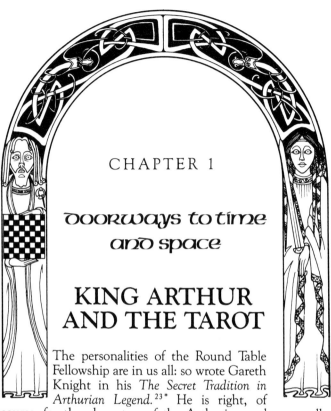

CHAPTER 1

ⱄoorⱳays to time and space

KING ARTHUR AND THE TAROT

The personalities of the Round Table Fellowship are in us all: so wrote Gareth Knight in his *The Secret Tradition in Arthurian Legend*.[23]* He is right, of course, for the characters of the Arthurian cycle are really archetypes of the highest order, having a reality far and above that of ordinary literary creations. The nature of their lives and adventures is always such that they perform archetypal actions. This is their mythic function, for the perform essential roles on behalf of the rest of humanity and this makes them suitable for esoteric work, for here such archetypal forces are codified and aligned with natural and inner world patterns.

The use of a literary creation with an esoteric system such as

*All reference numbers are keyed to the Bibliography (page 153).

the Tarot may seem extraordinary. Indeed, if the Arthurian legends *were* solely literary inventions we could not have created the *Arthurian Tarot*. It is because the stories about King Arthur and his court arise from much earlier levels — from the mythic and oral traditions of Britain — that we are able to trace the archetypal threads which keep the mythic web in shape.

The mythology of the Arthurian world is a cumulative one, drawing on native British tradition, Romano-British history, Celtic myth and medieval elaboration, with, latterly, additions from Tennyson, T. H. White, Charles Williams and numerous modern poets and novelists. For most people, the Arthurian world is permanently established in the Middle Ages by the conventions of Malory. But this formalization of the legends, while perhaps helping to preserve the Matter of Britain, as the Arthurian legends are known, has also obscured them in many ways.

It has been our task to help restore the mythic links between the earlier and later traditions so that in this way the mythic patterns underlying the Arthurian legend could provide us with the basis for the *Arthurian Tarot*. What began as a corpus of stories to be enjoyed by everyone is here depicted as the *Hallowquest*: a series of doorways into time and space.

That we are able to do this offers a verification, if not a vindication of the archetypal nature not only of the Tarot system but also of the Arthurian mythos. The universality of the Tarot needs no proving; neither for that matter does the power of the Arthurian stories to move, and to illuminate those who encounter them, in a universally acknowledged way.

The cards which form the *Hallowquest* are the result of long meditation. Nothing has been depicted because it seemed aesthetically pleasing or intellectually correct. We have gone back to the proto-Celtic roots of the mythos, drawing upon deeper Otherworldly and timeless qualities to produce the cards of the Greater Powers; while the land of Britain itself has been our inspiration in creating the cards of the Lesser Powers.

The symbolism which governs the whole pack is that of the Hallows themselves — the Sword, the Spear, the Grail and the

Stone which are emblematic of the elements of Air, Fire, Water and Earth, respectively, as well as being the objects of the _Hallowquest_ itself. This fourfold elemental correspondence is not only nearer to the spirit of the Celto-Arthurian mythos, but also central to an understanding of the Tarot. If we faithfully follow the way of the Four Hallows — the holy empowering objects of the inner quest — we will be given the regalia of the sovereign within each of us. We will no longer be wounded like the Grail King of legend, but made whole by the power of the elements.

Those readers who are attached to the medieval format of the Arthurian legends may be disappointed in not finding it depicted here. We hope that there is sufficient fusion between the so-called Dark Age Arthur and his more elaborate flowering as a medieval king, and that readers will persevere with the earlier images and find them rewarding. The Arthurian mythos is like a great tree planted in ancient soil: although everyone sees the branches, it is the roots which channel the earth's nourishment to the leaves and fruit upon it.

The Arthurian legends furnish an exciting and deeply moving symbology in which to operate, for they provide the mythic levels from which its themes and characters draw their life and potency. Without these qualities, the images do not step off the cards into the imagination, and unless they do so, the Tarot is a worthless system.

That the two systems of the Matter of Britain and the Tarot should work reciprocally is itself a wonder, as we discovered as we entered deeper into the hidden worldscape of the _Hallowquest_. There we encountered forces at once personal and universal in their application — as are all great archetypes. The characters and themes of the Arthurian court who came to represent the Greater and Lesser Powers (the Major and Minor Arcanas) stood forth ever more clearly as we worked. Though we knew, or felt we knew them already, as our work proceeded we came to know them more deeply in their essential format.

All this and more may be opened for us as we pass through

any of the 78 doorways of the *Hallowquest*. What we do with the knowledge we have gained is for us to decide, but whatever choice we make will most certainly be profound within the inscape of our lives.

GETTING TO KNOW THE HALLOWQUEST PACK

Without worrying about the meanings of each card or noticing the ways in which the cards vary from traditional packs, take the cards out of their box and scan each of the images in a relaxed way. Some will appeal to you straight away, others may repel you, while some may be baffling or unclear. Spread them out around you on the floor; play with them, make up stories by putting one card next to another at random. Each individual card has its mood, quality or feel, and these can be perceived without your having to look up the meanings.

In the next few weeks, try to handle the pack as much as possible. This handling will break the printed, laminated cards from the factory into your own personal set of symbols. Let the cards become familiar to your fingers and to your imaginative senses. Some books on the Tarot suggest all manner of arcane ways of making the Tarot special to you; if you want to protect the cards both physically and psychically by wrapping them in silk and placing them in a special box, then by all means do so, but it is not essential.

If you are going to do any serious work with these cards for yourself or others, you are going to have to learn their ascriptions very thoroughly. This process is an organic one which cannot be rushed.

Learning by rote can be very boring. Many of us learned multiplication tables this way, but not with any enthusiasm. The learning process must engage the imagination if it is to be effective. If you have a photographic memory then you might consider it an advantage to be able to 'snap' each card with your remembering eye, but this is not going to help much when you are reading for a querent with a set of complex needs. Single cards may have fixed meanings, but when they interrelate in a spread they modify their effect. Adaptability is the order of the exercise.

As you begin to work with the *Hallowquest* pack you will discover many correlations and meanings, even stories and other realizations arising from your research and use of the cards. The freshness and vitality of these discoveries are often swiftly lost and you may wish to record them in a workbook. Any loose-leaf folder will suffice, enabling you to rearrange and insert pages where and when you like. In this way you will be making the *Arthurian Tarot* your own.

The value of records or notes is much understated in the learning process. By writing down your discoveries immediately when things are going well for you, you will be able to refer to them again on the days when you feel depressed or discouraged. A record or workbook will also give a sense of shape and an idea of your progress.

Decide at the outset what kind of learning programme you want to follow: remember, you can be both systematic *and* creative. You may wish to start meditating or studying one card at a time until you work your way through the pack. In this case you can assign a number of pages in your workbook for each card on which to record your findings.

Study each card, noting down as you go your initial feelings or impressions. Now look up the meanings given to your card. These archetypal symbols are going to represent real life situations for any querents who consult you, so take time to imagine real situations or circumstances which that card might represent. For example: Greater Power XVIII, the Moon; this card represents the state of inner preparation and the cyclicity of growth. Several images will immediately occur to you: the growth of a child in the womb, just as is depicted in the card. But it might also represent a pregnant woman, the burgeoning of creative ideas, the receptivity for inspiration of all kinds. The cards will not always represent concrete objects or situations, but feelings, concepts or influences.

THE SHAPE OF THE HALLOWQUEST

In order to understand the way the *Arthurian Tarot* works, the following diagrams show the shape of the pack and its correspondences with traditional Tarot systems.

The Greater Powers

No.	Traditional Title	Hallowquest Title
0	The Fool	The Seeker
I	The Magician	Merlin
II	The High Priestess	The Lady of the Lake
III	The Empress	Guinevere
IV	The Emperor	Arthur
V	The Hierophant	Taliesin
VI	The Lovers	The White Hart
VII	The Chariot	Prydwen
VIII	Strength	Gawain
IX	The Hermit	The Grail Hermit
X	The Wheel of Fortune	The Round Table
XI	Justice	Sovereignty
XII	The Hanged Man	The Wounded King
XIII	Death	The Washer at the Ford
XIV	Temperance	The Cauldron
XV	The Devil	The Green Knight
XVI	The Tower	The Spiral Tower
XVII	The Star	The Star
XVIII	The Moon	The Moon
XIX	The Sun	The Sun
XX	The Last Judgement	The Sleeping Lord
XXI	The World	The Flowering of Logres

The Lesser Powers

The Four Hallow Suits and their Correspondences

Hallowquest Tarot	Traditional Tarot	Playing Cards	Season	Element	Colour
Sword	Swords	Spades	Spring	Air	Yellow
Spear	Wands	Clubs	Summer	Fire	Red
Grail	Cups	Hearts	Autumn	Water	Blue
Stone	Pentacles	Diamonds	Winter	Earth	Green

The Composition of the Hallow Suits

Aces	= the four Hallows of Celto-Arthurian tradition: the Sword, the Spear, the Grail and the Stone.
Cards 2-9	= the landscape of the Hallowquest through which the Seeker journeys.
Card 10	= one of the four Courts of the Hallows, represented by a castle.
Court Cards	= the Maiden, Knight, Queen and King of each Hallow castle.

REVERSED MEANINGS

You will notice that the *Arthurian Tarot* does not have any reversed meanings given. The reasons for this are both esoteric and practical. Every aspect of life has its dual quality or application. However, the archetypal or Otherworldly levels function differently for they are powers in their own right: they are neither good nor evil, beneficial or detrimental in their essence. They are non-dual. This is why we have called the Major and Minor Arcana 'The Greater and Lesser Powers.'

The reversed or contrary meanings are therefore implicit in each card by virtue of their placement in a spread, and we have left it up to the discernment of the *Hallowquest* user to find these, where they are appropriate.

There is no virtue in attempting to stare at a reversed card which the artist has drafted to be comprehended in an upright position, since the potency and symbolism are thereby lost. If cards turn up in reversed positions when you are reading them, turn them the right way up, considering, as you do so, the implication of that card and its interrelation with the others in more detail. If you are using them for story-telling, myth-making or any of the other creative exercises then do not hesitate to turn them upright and work with them that way.

If you have been used to working with reversed meanings in other packs you may wish to do so with the *Arthurian Tarot*. If you wish to explore the possibility further, then you could do no better than refer to Gail Fairfield's *Choice Centred Tarot*,[7] which will give you ideas on how you can adapt the *Hallowquest* pack.

If you are using one card alone, then it is always 'neutral'. When the cards are placed side by side certain combinations automatically call into being a response which will be different, depending on the querent, the reader and the cards chosen.

THE LANGUAGE OF SYMBOLISM

The Tarot is a pictorial language, a symbology which has a number of uses, only one of which is fortune-telling. You will find many different ways to utilize the pack in our book *Hallowquest: Tarot Magic and the Arthurian Mysteries*. It is possible that you never conceived of the Tarot as being anything other than a divinatory system. If you read the chapters on meditation, ritual and story-telling and try some of the exercises from *Hallowquest*, we hope that you will be pleasantly surprised and excited by the potential of the cards.

Symbolic systems are not confined to men or women only, to esotericists or magicians only. The wisdom they contain extends to all who can respond to their messages and meanings. So while the *Hallowquest* deck draws its inspiration from the cultural mythos of Britain, of which the Arthurian legends are but a part, this does not limit its application to merely one time or place. Since you have purchased this pack, you are undoubtedly interested in the Arthurian world and its deeper levels, but the *Hallowquest* is not reserved solely for Arthurian experts or people born in Britain.

The inner Britain, called Logres in the early texts, is part of the Otherworldly reality which is available to all. Tibet has its Shambhalla, Greece its Hesperides, but Britain has its Avalon. These timeless realities are always available, since they are the mystical repositories of wisdom and ancestral lore; they transcend the barriers of race, culture and time. Anyone who has responded to the Arthurian legends, will find the *Hallowquest* usable as a mythic system of understanding. The Arthurian Powers and their totems will lead *Hallowquest* users to discover these very Otherworldly levels of wisdom for themselves.

It is important when dealing with symbolic languages to understand that they have many levels of application and that, in their pure form, they exist in their own right. The images and characters depicted in the *Arthurian Tarot* represent archetypal or Otherworldly powers. It is inappropriate to apply the archetypal roles on a purely human plane, because this confuses symbolic levels. The Arthurian or Greater Powers do not represent either divine or human energies. They may be rightly described as daemons. Daemons are not demons, but the inner guiding agencies which are neither incarnate humans nor disincarnate gods. They are the inner voices of our dreams, our guardian angel or inner companion spirit. The language they speak is symbolically exact and authoritatively voiced. To expect them to speak of our very mundane concerns is as foolish as to imagine that an angel might advise us financially.

The Greater Powers speak of deeper and more archetypal matters than the payment of bills or the unhappy relationships we may have. When the *Hallowquest* deck is used in divination, the appearance of the Greater Powers signifies a more urgent voice, reminding us that even we mortals have our part to sing in the larger harmony of Creation. They urge us to recall that we too are part of the great weaving pattern of the earth's fabric and make us look more closely at the overall pattern which our lives are making. The Lesser Powers speak more plainly and mundanely; they speak about our general direction and the ways in which we both make our path more difficult and how we might make it smoother.

The method of reading the pictorial language of this symbolic system cannot be taught. It is like the language of the birds, the mysterious ability to remember that which we have never consciously known, the ability to pick out of the air the patterns and shapings of a greater reality. This is part of the learning and interpretative process which you will acquire or not, depending on whether you are able to align your willingness to learn with an equal receptivity to understand.

The *Hallowquest* Tarot possesses its own set of teachers in the shape of the Greater Powers: listen to them carefully and you too will learn to speak, read and understand the language of the Otherworld.

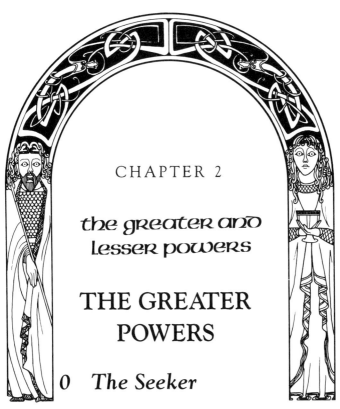

CHAPTER 2

the greater and lesser powers

THE GREATER POWERS

0 *The Seeker*

Description: In a wasted landscape, the Seeker sets out on his journey. Dressed in ragged clothing and barefoot, he steps off a high place and takes the rainbow path, impelled by the song of the Birds of Rhiannon which fly above him.

Background: All quests begin with a question: 'Why are things like this?' This is a variation on the famous Grail question: 'Whom does the Grail serve?' This inquisitiveness is the hallmark of the Seeker, who is not content to let imbalances remain unchallenged. The Hallow seeker is impelled by a deep urgency to know and experience: to find the world's healing and to seek for a personal direction. This path is both journey and goal.

o the seeker

Potentially, every Seeker is the Grail winner — a role which is open to women and men alike. The legends tell of Peredur or Perceval whose desire for experience of the world leads him into becoming one of Arthur's knights and eventually in his being the 'One Who Frees the Waters', as the Grail winner is known. Yet he starts as the Perfect Fool, the one whose divine unwisdom uncouples the chains of time and space.[58, 30]

The Seeker's steps upon the quest are directed by his communion with the Otherworldly messengers whose song sounds in his ears. The Birds of Rhiannon betoken joy, sorrow, and awareness of the Otherworld, for they sing eternally on the Tree of Life in the Land of Promise.

And yet to gain the Otherworldly Hallows, the Seeker must travel the physical world for it is only thus that the Hallows will empower and balance the land. It is so that the Seeker travels light, humbly and in a guise which will attract least attention to his quest. The Seeker, like the Fool and the poorman, despised and overlooked, can go everywhere. So it is with our own quest. It is better to travel without the weight of fixed ideas; only so can the free flow of our destiny be unwound. Those who explore the inner worlds cannot retain their preconceived ideas of themselves: dignity and self-esteem must be left at home, for this is a journey which will change us.

The Seeker can ask questions and weigh answers, free to juxtapose whatever ideas come his or her way. And this is the rainbow path, the way of experience upon which the Seeker learns how to heal what is broken, balance what is imbalanced, align what is out of alignment.

Archetypal Meaning: The Seeker represents all who go on a spiritual quest as well as those who seek for the healing of the Wasteland. He is the wise fool who embarks on his quest without a thought for the consequences or those left behind, for this inner journey can only be undertaken singly. His wisdom is to unconsciously follow the path to the Grail and the healing of Logres.

Divinatory Meaning: Childlike trust; divine discontent; carefree enthusiasm; protection; the folly to be wise; optimism; adventure; spontaneity; youthful energy; longing to find one's heart's desire.

I Merlin

Description: Merlin stands before a stone table on which is laid a map of Britain. The four Hallows, the Sword, the Spear, the Grail and the Stone Chessboard lie upon it. Above his

head a red and white dragon intertwine. To his right is the dark, crumbling tower of Vortigern; while to his left is his Otherworldly dwelling with many doors and windows.

Background: The early life of Merlin is often forgotten, but it is of prime importance for understanding his role in the Arthurian cycle. Merlin was born of an earthly mother and an Otherworldly father, thus establishing him as a prime mover and mediator between the two realities of this world and the Otherworld. [70]

In early legend he is called Myrddin Emrys. [53] As a child he was brought before Vortigern, the unworthy King of Britain. Vortigern had attempted to build a tower in which he might take refuge from his enraged subjects, but it fell down three times. His magicians said that it would remain standing only if the blood of a child who had no father was sprinkled on the foundations. But Merlin confounded the magicians and showed that the cause of the tower's collapse was because of the two dragons which warred continuously beneath it. The red one signified the Britons and the white one the Saxons whom Vortigern had settled in Britain. [9]

According to Geoffrey of Monmouth, Merlin prepares the way for the Pendragons, for Arthur and his father, Uther, [8] and although later texts speak of Merlin's imprisonment at the hands of Nimuë or Vivienne, who is said to have enticed him into revealing his magic through love of her, a closer investigation of the earlier texts reveals that Merlin's retirement is a voluntary one. His sister, Gwendydd or Ganieda, builds for him an observatory having 70 doors and windows, from which he may view the heavens. [70] This legend is closely associated with an oral tradition concerning Merlin's guardianship of Britain which is called *Clas Myrddin* or Merlin's Enclosure. Further legend credits Merlin with retiring to Bardsey Island, to a Glass House, in which he keeps the 13 treasures of Britain. [78]

Archetypal Meaning: Merlin is the inner herald of dreams, relaying the messages of the Otherworld in symbolic form. He is also prophet and seer. He enables the manifestation of events which lie in embryo through his mastery over the four elements, although he does not manipulate events. His real magic lies in his balanced mediation of inner and outer worlds.

Divinatory Meaning: The impulse of creation; imaginative insight; mastery through disciplined skill; initiative; self-confidence; perception on all levels; alignment to and free flow with one's life patterns.

II The Lady of the Lake

Description: On the middle of an island in the middle of a lake sits the Lady of the Lake on a throne of reeds. She holds a sword and a book, while at her feet is a basket. Beside her is a crane.

Background: Throughout the Arthurian legends, Otherworldly women guide and instruct Arthur and his court. During the Middle Ages, these many aspects of the Goddess splintered into numerous maidens, wronged ladies and widows. If we return to the earlier texts we find that rather than a bevy of damsels who need knightly assistance to gain their rights, certain powerful women of great stature appear at crucial times to aid and assist the knights.

ii the lady of the lake

The Lady of the Lake stems from a very circuitous lineage of such women, chief of whom is Morgen or Morgan, described as the daughter of *Rex Avallonis* or the king of Avalon, as the sister of Arthur, or as queen of a ninefold sisterhood in her own right.[19, 41] It is she who tends Arthur's wounds after the Battle of Camlan and in whose charge he remains, in Otherworldly time, until he is called again.

But the role of healer is not the only one which the Lady of the Lake fulfils. She is also fosterer and initiator into knowledge. Traditionally among the Celtic races, women warriors trained boys in the arts of combat. In all the earlier stories about the Grail winner or champion of the Hallows, the boy is fostered in the Otherworld. Fosterage was a custom prevalent among the Celts, stabilizing the tribe and establishing bonds of love and mutual obligation.

The unknown boyhood of Arthur, which the later texts say was spent in the care of Sir Ector of the Forest Sauvage, may indeed have been with the Lady of the Lake in one of her guises in the lost stories of the oral tradition.[41] It is from her that he gains his sword, Excalibur, and to her island that he is later borne to be healed of his wounds.

Medieval French tradition tells of Lancelot's upbringing with the Lady of the Lake. She raises him in accordance to the code of the Otherworld, as well as in courtesy and combat. She both names and arms him in accordance with the principles of Celtic story wherein the hero has to earn his name by his deeds.[80]

Elements of the Lady of the Lake as fosterer are also apparent in the story of Taliesin. (See p.30.)

Archetypal Meaning: The Lady of the Lake is the primal initiator into Otherworldly knowledge. She is foster-mother, mistress of wisdom and inspirer. She empowers the seeker after truth, and acts as the conscience of the initiate. She may appear in many forms to admonish, guide and instruct. She is the guardian of inner wisdom.

Divinatory Meaning: Esoteric knowledge; enlightenment;

inspiration; wisdom; the ability to impart instruction; counsel; psychic healing; learning.

III Guinevere

Description: Guinevere sits spinning in a meadow. A white cow grazes nearby.

Background: Guinevere seems to exist in most people's minds as the faithless wife of Arthur whose guilty love of Lancelot caused the downfall of the Round Table. Such a picture is not consistent with the early figure of Guinevere who, as Gwenhwyfar, is described as 'one of the three, gentle, gold-torqued ladies of Britain',[78] whose integrity upholds the honour of Arthur's court and whose beauty reflects the fertile face of the land.

The accusations of infidelity levelled against Guinevere are without foundation in the early traditions which certainly speak of her abduction by a series of men, including Medrawt (Mordred), and Melwas.[24] It is not until Chrétien de Troyes' *Le Chevalier de la Charrette* in the late twelfth century that we find Lancelot in the role of rescuer, though not yet as the active lover of Guinevere.[4]

Putting the evidence together, we find that Guinevere aligns to an archetype identified as the Flower Bride — the Otherworldly woman, often a representative of the Goddess of Sovereignty — who becomes the consort of a king. Her role is to manifest, in her own person, the harmony between king and land. But if she is not matched on every level by a reciprocal love from her consort then she looks for a champion to challenge the king and remind him of his duties towards his queen and the land which she represents.

She is indeed championed by many knights, including the Grail winner, Peredur (Perceval), and Gereint; they both avenge Guinevere in separate incidents when she is insulted by an unnamed knight, who is possibly of Otherworldly provenance.

Perhaps the clearest key to her original role is found in the Triad which describes her as the Triple Gwenhwyfar — as three women, each of whom was supposed to be the spouse of Arthur. Celtic tradition has a strongly developed sense of triplicity which extends to the aspects of a particular archetype or deity. Guinevere, as the Flower Bride, along with the Lady of the Lake as the foster-mother, and the Washer at the Ford as the Cailleach or hag, make up the composite manifestation of the Goddess of Sovereignty in the Arthurian world.[41]

Archetypal Meaning: Guinevere as the Empress of Logres (the inner Britain) creates the conditions for growth, establishing peace and contentment. She spins a thread of inner concord which is woven into the fabric of the land and its people. She imparts sensitivity to nature and harmonious awareness to all life.

Divinatory Meaning: Energy in creative growth; material and spiritual wealth; fulfilment; beauty, abundance; fertility; motherhood; health; harmony.

IV *Arthur*

Description: Arthur sits in a stone chair on a mountain-top.

The draco standard flies behind him and Excalibur lies across his knees. A Cornish chough perches near the throne.

Background: The figure of Arthur is a complex one made of many strata of tradition. Most people are familiar with Arthur the medieval king and champion of Christendom, but behind this there lie other, equally valid personas: Dark Age battle lord, Romano-British chieftain or Celtic god-hero. The Arthur of the _Hallowquest_ deck is a mixture of all three of these designations.

The primary feature of Arthur's role is his guardianship and defence of the land, which takes us into the realm of mythic reality where the historical sixth-century battle leader is subsumed in a welter of divine and heroic traditions. As William Blake wrote, 'The stories of Arthur are the acts of Albion'. This perhaps explains the curious rippling out of the legends surrounding him, for around Arthur constellate the Greater Powers of the Arthurian world. From being a lone heroic figure he gathers about him an actual as well as a withdrawn court, in which knights, ladies, heroes, gods and goddesses are numbered.

This great panoply of archetypes is not immediately apparent from a cursory reading of medieval Arthurian romances whose complex enlacements cross and recross the original tradition confusingly. In the later romances, Arthur is a figurehead, based squarely upon the model of Christian kingship; he no longer engages in adventures in his own right — these are performed by the knights of his court. He is represented by numerous champions, chief of which is Gawain. Turning to the earlier stories, we find that Arthur leads his army into the underworld of Annwn; he rescues Gwenhwyfar (Guinevere) from her faery abductor; he encounters the Goddess of Sovereignty and takes the empowerment of the Hallows.[41] He is an active, initiating leader whose care is for his people and the land.

The divine or heroic elements within his role are amplified by tradition. Whenever he attempts to depart from his kingly responsibilities within the legends, or to live a life of his own, he comes to grief. Where he fulfils the duties of a king, he is given the support and assistance of the Goddess of Sovereignty. She is his foster-mother who instructs him in wisdom, she brings him to the kingship, she provides him with a wife and eventually receives him to her again in the Isle of Avalon from whence prophecy says he will come again to defend the land once more.

Archetypal Meaning: Arthur is the Emperor of Logres, the Pendragon. He draws together the resources of his land and welds them into a kingdom full of strength and vitality. His creative energy is fuelled by close Otherworld contact through the mediation of Sovereignty (XI).

Divinatory Meaning: Leadership; authoritative energy; the wielding of power for the good of all; will-power; organization; courage; responsible love; fatherhood; dynamism.

V Taliesin

Description: Taliesin sits in a firelit hall. He tells the story of his initiatory transformations to two children who sit at his feet listening intently. The golden links of tradition pass from his hands into theirs.

o taliesin

Background: The legend of the transformations of Gwion Bach into the poet Taliesin is told in the *Hanes Taliesin*.[30] We read how Gwion was set to tend the magical cauldron of Ceridwen. This cauldron of inspiration was intended for the drinking of Afagddu, Ceridwen's son, who was so ill-favoured that his mother wished to compensate for his lack of natural beauty by the gift of wisdom. However, young Gwion's fingers were splashed with liquid from the cauldron and, to cool them, he thrust them into his mouth and so acquired the cauldron's wisdom for himself. Realizing his own danger through his new-won omniscience, Gwion transformed himself into a hare but Ceridwen pursued in the form of a hound; he changed into a fish and she into an otter; he changed into a bird and she into a hawk; lastly, he became a grain of wheat and she scrabbled him up into her crop as a hen. He was reborn of her womb nine months later as the infant Taliesin.[30]

This story is a parable of bardic initiation in which the young poet establishes his essential links with the Otherworld, in which all levels of reality and wisdom are available. By means of his totemic associations with the different birds, beasts and fish — each of whom represent a level of knowledge — the poet is able to participate simultaneously in every part of creation in an omniscient way. He knows what has happened in the deep past and what will happen in the times to come.

Although Taliesin is primary chief bard to Elphin in this legend, he is associated closely with Arthur in other texts. According to the ninth-century poem, *Preiddeu Annwn*, [44] Taliesin accompanies Arthur on his quest to Annwn; while, in Geoffrey of Monmouth's *Vita Merlini*, [9] Taliesin helps Merlin bear Arthur to Avalon to be healed by the Goddess, Morgen.

The greatest repository of lore is to be found within the writings which constitute *The Book of Taliesin*. [59] This takes the form of intricate, gnomic poetry packed with references to myth, legend and magic. The lists of 'I have beens . . .' in which the poet refers to events throughout history at which he was present, reflect a mystical understanding of creation seldom found elsewhere.

Taliesin is the guardian of tradition. By means of his insights he is able to impart wisdom by means of song and story so that the youngest child can hear and understand. It is by such means that the mythic impact of the Arthurian Powers has been transmitted to our own century, for the living links of tradition pass into our keeping. While there will always be special guardians, traditional lore is embodied by the people who tell and listen to the stories.

Those who seek earnestly and sincerely for wisdom will encounter Taliesin who, though his real dwelling place is the 'region of the summer stars', is nevertheless ready to aid the seeker and help him or her to contact the living wisdom of the Otherworld.

Archetypal Meaning: Taliesin is the guardian of tradition. By song and story, by prophecy and far memory, he can instruct and guide the seeker. He is an interpreter as well as a teacher, well able to represent images to the receptive mind and forge connections in the waiting heart.

Divinatory Meaning: Tradition; revelation; inspiration; insight; preservation of heritage; initiation; advice or counsel; transformation of the mundane into the spiritual.

of the white hart

VI   The White Hart

Description: In a forest clearing we see Gereint out hunting transfixed at the sight of Enid, who sees the White Hart coming towards them.

Background: The lovers depicted here are Gereint and Enid. Their story appears in the _Mabinogion_[30] as well as in Chrétien de Troyes' _Erec and Enid_[4] Gereint is a knight of Arthur's court who seeks to avenge an insult done to Guinevere by Edern ap Nudd. He pursues Edern with neither arms nor armour, but is given these by Earl Yniwl, who has been dispossessed by Edern. The only way Gereint can avenge the insult to Guinevere is to fight Edern at the Sparrowhawk contest — a tournament in which a kestrel is awarded to the knight who successfully overcomes all challengers. The contest rules state that each combatant must fight for his lady's honour, and Gereint has no lady. He asks to champion Enid, Yniwl's daughter. He beats Edern, wins the sparrowhawk and wins Enid as his wife.

The hunting of the White Hart — a ritual hunt which is the preserve of the Pendragons only — takes place in Gereint's absence. Arthur himself captures the beast and cuts off its head; the custom is that the head should be awarded to the fairest lady, but Guinevere delays the disposal of the head until Gereint returns with Enid. Guinevere takes Enid under her protection and prepares her for marriage to Gereint. The head of the White Hart is then awarded to Enid.

The testing of Gereint and Enid's love in the ensuing story is very much as a result of the foregoing incident. The appearance of the White Hart in Celto-Arthurian literature usually heralds a change in the order of things, for it is a messenger of the Goddess of Sovereignty whose Otherworldly influence leads the lovers in this story into further testing and many severe trials of their affection.

Gereint's rather superficial affection for Enid is deepened, while her unworldly idealism is assimilated into a more practical manifestation of love. The White Hart represents the call of the Otherworld to compassion and commitment to the spiritual quest. The attainment of its head is a royal or initiatic task which only king, champion or lover can undertake.

For a fuller breakdown of this story see *Arthur and the Sovereignty of Britain*. [41]

Archetypal Meaning: The White Hart is the Otherworldly messenger into spiritual adventure and the purity of love. Those who hunt it are drawn deeper into themselves and made aware of the pure power of love to overcome all obstacles. It also represents the silver chain of sexual desire which is between men and women, but it also enhances that desire into love that is strong as death.

Divinatory Meaning: Love, both sexual and spiritual; the vision of inner beauty; emotional ties; trust; the marriage of minds and hearts; platonic friendship; fulfilment of desire.

VII   Prydwen

Description: Arthur's ship, Prydwen, sails into the entrance of the Underworld, Annwn. From the mast-head flies the White Boar standard.

Background: One of the earliest British poems, *Preiddeu Annwn*[29] or *The Spoils of Anwn* tells of Arthur's journey to the Underworld to win the Hallows of Britain, specifically the cauldron of Pen Annwn. He sails on his ship, Prydwen, with three companies of men. The poem tells of the arduous journey in which they pass the seven caers or towers of the Underworld, taking with them the cauldron of plenty. It relates the releasing of the youth who is held prisoner there, who is a type of Mabon, the divine youth of Celto-Arthurian legend. (See p.58.) Prydwen returns to Britain, but only seven of Arthur's company return to speak of their adventures.

This refrain 'except seven, none return,' is a feature of another exploit to do with a cauldron in which the legendary Bran the Blessed goes to Ireland to rescue his sister, Branwen, from ill-treatment at the hands of her husband, Matholwch, the Irish king. In the ensuing battle, the Irish reanimate their dead warriors in the miraculous cauldron of rebirth; they out-number the British so badly that only seven return from that adventure. Legend says that Taliesin was one of each of the two companies of seven.[30]

This almost forgotten incident in Arthur's career once formed part of a greater cycle of stories in which Arthur was the prime hero; the voyage in Prydwen is Arthur's *immram* or

Otherworldly journey, comparable with the Irish *immrama* of Maelduine and Bran mac Febal.[16] The raid on Annwn is closely associated with another story in which Arthur pursues the giant boar Twrch Trwyth, between whose ears are certain Otherworldly treasures. In this story he also voyages on Prydwen, to Ireland — which we can see as analogous to the Underworld — and does battle with the boar in person, sustaining many grievous injuries as well as a considerable loss of men.[44]

The overlays between the voyage of Arthur and that of Bran suggest a closer mythical association. There is a Triad which tells how Bran's head was buried at the White Mount (the Tower of London) in order to act as a Palladium against invasion. The ravens which are kept at the present day Tower are a reminder of this (Bran means raven). But the Triad goes on to relate how Arthur, wishing to have no other defence but his own, disinterred the head. We perceive here a gleam of an earlier tradition in which Arthur's voyage to Annwn was to win the Treasures of Britain, the Hallows themselves, from the hands of Pen Annwn, the Lord of the Underworld — a role perhaps fulfilled by Bran himself.

Archetypal Meaning: Prydwen represents the Otherworldly journey which is undertaken by all seekers, so that the inner life becomes the basis for a sound outer life. In this card, faith in one's abilities and the true strength of one's determination are tested to the utmost. By the balancing of hard work with periods of contemplative insight, victory is gained.

Divinatory Meaning: Victory; self-confidence; self-discipline; the harnessing of abilities towards a great purpose; tests and trials; achievement; travel; determination; courage.

VIII   Gawain

Description: Under the midday sun, Gawain stands armed, ready for combat, at a ford near a pass. Above him a hawk hovers.

Background: Gawain or Gwalchmai, as he appears in the earliest stories, is the prime champion of Arthur who is his uncle as well as his king. Later tradition robs Gawain of much of his courageous integrity, making him a boorish lout. However, earlier tradition establishes him as the most courteous knight of Arthur's court, one who is most involved with the championship of the land.[51]

This is evident from his close association with the Goddess, whose many representatives he encounters. Chief among these is Lady Ragnell who, in the medieval story of _Gawain and Ragnell_[18] appears as the Loathly Lady whom Gawain has to marry in order to save Arthur from a terrible foe. It is Gawain and not Arthur who in this story kisses the hideous representative of Sovereignty; Ragnell then assumes her real guise of a beautiful woman. Although we have only the medieval evidence of this story, we know from Irish parallels that the Goddess of Sovereignty's champions establish a pattern of behaviour which is emulated by Gawain.[51]

Gawain's championship of Arthur's kingdom may be interestingly envisioned in the light of Celtic kingship customs which established a _tanaiste_ or likely successor during a king's lifetime. In this way, the tribe had a nominated successor in the event of the king's sudden death. The _tanaiste's_ duties entailed keeping a close eye on his future inheritance. As Arthur's nephew, Gawain has a double right to this role, since he is the son of Arthur's sister — she is called Morgause in the later texts, but the earlier ones call her Anna,[8] Gwyar[41] or Morcades.[51] The Celtic royal bloodline descended through the mother's side, since the royal woman of a clan was her tribe's sovereignty.

Gawain is perhaps best known for his exploits within the medieval story of *Sir Gawain and the Green Knight*,[18] in which he successfully combats the Green Knight in a contest which demands both physical strength and inner resourcefulness. (See p.51.) Traditionally, Gawain's strength increases up to midday when it starts to wane. This is perhaps reflected in his original name — Gwalchmai — or Hawk of May.

Archetypal Meaning: Gawain represents the balanced strength of the initiate who is both physically healthy and spiritually whole. In him the polarities of life are resolved and balanced: male and female, strength and compassion, severity and mercy. He is the knightly extension of Arthur (IV) himself, fulfilling the will of the King and loyal to the Goddess of Sovereignty in the land of Logres.

Divinatory Meaning: Self-discipline; enduring strength; balanced exercise of one's abilities; health of mind, body and spirit; moral certitude, without self-righteousness; courage to accept challenges; fortitude.

IX The Grail Hermit

Description: A forest clearing in which the Grail Hermit has his dwelling. He sits outside his bothy, writing in his book. His flowering staff grows nearby, while on an engraved menhir a dove roosts.

Background: The Grail tradition in Arthurian legend springs from two sources: from the native stories about the cauldron and various regenerative vessels, and from the apocryphal

IX THE GRAIL HERMIT

stories which grew up from the amalgamation of pagan and Christian traditions.

In both of these, a kingly hermit plays a central part. Medieval legend, drawing upon traditions about Bran the Blessed and the sacred wounding of the king, portrayed Brons as the Grail guardian.[45] Christian tradition supplied Joseph of Arimathea and the lineage of hermits who spring from his family. Venerable tradition states that Joseph brought the infant Christ to Britain on one of his trading voyages. Similar legends relate that the relics of Christ were brought by Joseph to Glastonbury, where he founded the first church.

These relics have been variously described as the two cruets which contained the blood and water from the side of Christ, or, alternatively, the Cup of the Last Supper. Both traditions merged, and in the fullness of time they were grafted onto the indigeous Grail legends.

The Grail hermits of Arthurian legend fulfil a necessary task in the quest, admonishing the lazy, explaining the significance of the wonders which are encountered and providing welcome rest and shelter from the rigours of the search.

The seamless garment of tradition has wrought the twin realities of the pagan and Christian visions into a dynamic and potent mythos. For while the Celtic cauldron is the object of individual kings and heroes, all people are included within the dispensation of the Christian Grail — the finding of which does not necessitate being of a royal or holy lineage. The combined Grail tradition is open to all people of good will and intent, who are invited to go and search for the life-giving cup. The old kingly sacrifice is transmuted into a once and for all time redemptive sacrifice by the Son of Light, who, by his incarnation as a human being, brings all peoples within his own bloodline, by virtue of the Blessed Virgin's own humanity which he himself assumes in order to die and so overcome death.

This mystery is at the heart of the Grail legends and is implicit within the mythos of the Celtic god, Mabon — whose name was sometimes interchangeable with that of Christ in British tradition. The Grail Hermit frequently features as the co-fosterer, with the Lady of the Lake, of the Grail winner.

Archetypal Meaning: The Grail Hermit represents the keeper and transmitter of esoteric lore. Neither Druid nor priest, as hermit he mediates the functions of both. His book is opened to all who go on quests. It warns them of the dangers and terrors which await them, but it also comforts and sustains those who lose their way on the path of spiritual renewal. His dove goes on before to guide seekers, while his staff steadies their failing steps.

Divinatory Meaning: Guidance; spiritual truth; illumination; wisdom; counsel — especially from an older or wiser person; introspection; a necessary space for reassessment; inner companionship; maturity; the voice of conscience or one's guardian angel/spirit.

X   The Round Table

Description: We see through the pupil of a hawk's eye a great plain on which is a henge of great stones, within this is a circle of swords. Above the henge is the Round Table. Above the Round Table is a circle of stars within which is a crystal cup.

x the ROUND table

Background: The Fellowship of the Round Table is at the heart of the medieval Arthurian legends. It inspired many historical orders of chivalry, contributing to the civilization of Europe during the Middle Ages, though, as with Fellowship described by Malory and others, these were not always consistent to the ideals of Christian compassion. The concept of a round table at which knights sit to relate their deeds and to regulate the laws of the land by their personal vigilance and action has descended into modern times where many social and welfare organizations have adopted it as their symbol.

The Round Table signifies a place of meeting and council and is a microcosm of the land itself where its representatives sit. Whatever is planned, discussed and experienced at the Table is manifested throughout the land.

The first meeting places and assembly points were probably the stone circles, such as Stonehenge, which Geoffrey of Monmouth says was magically transported by Merlin from Ireland as a memorial for Uther Pendragon.[8] Such legends are not without foundation, for we know that such megalithic monuments were indeed the focus of seasonal assembly. It is Merlin also who speaks of the making of the Round Table after the fashion of earlier tables, including the Table of the Last Supper, within the _Didot Perceval_.[58] He speaks there also of a third table which was made by Joseph of Arimathea — the Table of the Grail.

We see here these three tables superimposed one above the other. The stone circle of ancient sacred assembly, the Round Table of the medieval Arthurian legend, and the starry circle which is the gathering point for the disincarnate archetypes who mediate the powers of the Grail. When all three tables are aligned, then all levels of life are likewise harmonized with the cosmic laws governing our world.

Archetypal Meaning: The Round Table represents the stability of eternal laws which manifest in every age and cycle; to earthly perception these laws seem to be changeable and unpredictable, yet they follow certain cosmic patterns. Those who sit at the Round Table are subject to these laws and adapt themselves continuously to their manifestation.

Divinatory Meaning: Evolution; cyclic change; sequential patterns which result from any action; adaptation; incarnation or manifestation of a project; the passing of a concept, project or relationship to another phase; cosmic law or karma.

XI Sovereignty

Description: The Goddess of Sovereignty sits beside a spring.

XI SOVEREIGNTY

In her hands is the four-sided cup of truth. At her feet is an ermine.

Background: We have already heard much about Sovereignty in the backgrounds of the other Arthurian Powers. She is the epicentre about which the Arthurian legends revolve, for she is the Goddess of the Land and whatever affects the land causes changes in her. For this reason she is very difficult to discern among the later texts, for in her many guises she is scattered throughout the Matter of Britain.

She is called Sovereignty because this gift of royalty lies in her gift. All candidates for kingship must encounter her and accept her challenge. Usually she takes the form of a Cailleach or hag who demands a kiss from the hero; if he kisses her without revulsion, she will turn into her maiden aspect, often becoming his Flower Bride. (See p.27.) She will only accept the worthiest candidate to be king: he must be truthful, compassionate, just, courageous, and loyal to the land and its peoples. She will not accept anyone who is a self-serving individual given to lies and prevarication, just as she will not accept a blemished man — one who is physically imperfect.

Arthur encounters her in many forms, but usually within the persons of Guinevere, Morgan, Morcades and the Lady of the Lake. We lack the main stories of his encounters because these have become attached to his champions, Gawain, Perceval and others.

It is within the Grail legends that Sovereignty can be clearly seen as the Grail Maiden, who bears the regenerative cup; she appears also as the Queen of the Hallows in *Peredur*;[30] while, in her aspect of hag, she appears as the Grail Messenger or Hideous Damsel whose admonitory guidance brings the Grail winner to his goal.

In Celtic tradition, the Goddess of Sovereignty gives three drinks from her cup, purveying the white milk of fostering, the red drink of lordship and the dark drink of forgetfulness. These she offers successively in her aspects as Foster-Mother, Consort and Renewer.[41]

The four-sided cup of truth held by Sovereignty here is that of truth and justice: if three falsehoods are said over it it will shatter in pieces; but if three truths are said over it, it will reunite.

Archetypal Meaning: Sovereignty represents the inherent unity of the King and the land. She also stands for just and truthful dealings among all peoples. Whoever does not uphold the laws and customs of the land in their true spirit, is responsible for eroding the influence of the Goddess of Sovereignty. Like the earth itself, she must be respected.

Divinatory Meaning: Justice; equity; rightful rule; vindication of integrity; perception of motives; fair exchange; honest relationships; good measure; balanced reaction.

XII The Wounded King

Description: In a forest clearing hung with banners, the Wounded King lies on a bed. By his side is a hound; at his feet is a stone.

Background: The Wounded King appears in the Grail legends as its disempowered guardian. His unhealing wounds keep him in continual suffering and he is unable to be healed

XII the wounded king

until the Grail winner has achieved the redemptive vessel. Most people are familiar with this figure from Wagner's opera *Parzifal* where he is called the Fisher King. Wagner drew from Wolfram von Eschenbach's reworking of the French Grail romances[79] which in turn derive from British oral traditions.

The wounds of the King are reflected in the Wasteland which his kingdom has become: only the Grail can heal them both. It appears in the Wounded King's hall as a redemptive vision, usually as part of the procession of the Hallows which are borne in after the meal. But the Grail cannot do its work unless a worthy champion comes and asks the Grail question: 'What does this signify?' or 'Whom does the Grail serve?'

The asking of this question demonstrates that the seeker is aware of the wounds of the king and the wasting of the land, and truly desires to heal them both. It is only so that the Grail quest is activated.

But why is the King wounded in the first place? This question takes us into the deep mythos of the land. The medieval romances speak of the Dolorous Blow, by which Balin wounds King Pelles with the Lance of Longinus, thus causing the Wasteland.[31] But this is but one side of the story. We may cite Celtic kingship customs whereby a blemished or maimed king was forced to abdicate in favour of a more worthy candidate from the tribe. It was felt that an imperfect ruler could not worthily represent his people, for the king had to reflect the fertility of the land in his own person: a maimed king meant a barren land.

Mythically, we can see that the guardianship of the Hallows is itself a formidable task which the king can only maintain if he co-operates with the Otherworld. This relationship between the worlds is symbolized by his mystical marriage to the land, to the Goddess of Sovereignty herself. His vows of kingship to the people are in effect his marriage vows to Sovereignty, from whom he holds the Hallows in trust. If he breaks his binding oath, imbalances appear in his kingdom. The medieval romances show how clearly this is reflected in the career of Arthur himself who virtually becomes a Wounded

King because of his disempowerment: Guinevere gives her affections to Lancelot and so the kingdom's unity is shattered.

The Grail winner is potentially the new king, for he quests for the Hallows and, by his achievement of the Grail, he is able to heal the Wounded King. His Grail quest has brought him into relationship with the Otherworld, with Sovereignty and, ultimately, with the guardianship of the land. So although the Wounded King is healed, he does not remain the guardian of the Hallows: the Grail winner continues to maintain this role.

The origins of the Wounded King's sacrifice are deeply rooted in a prehistoric tradition by which the tribe's leader dies for his people. One such ruler is Bran the Blessed who, in Celtic tradition, is beheaded by his followers who then bury the head to repel invasion. Bran descended into medieval Grail tradition as Brons, the Fisher King — a title which arises from the confusion between the two similar French words pécheur (sinner) and pêcheur (fisher).

The Wounded King depicted here derives from the folk carol, *The Corpus Christi Carol*, where the wounds of the king are related to the redemptive sacrifice of Christ in a perfect fusion of ancient and Christian tradition.

Archetypal Meaning: The Wounded King represents the redemptive sacrifice of the Grail mysteries. His sufferings bring wisdom and insight, not only for himself but for his people. His is a willing sacrifice, not a gratuitous holocaust of blood. It is enjoined upon all seekers to ask the Grail question in whatever situation they find themselves: 'What is this about?' 'How may I remedy this?' The answer to these questions is the service of the Grail. There are many answers.

Divinatory Meaning: Wisdom gained through hardship and experience; spiritual insight; commitment to inner principles; the pain and misunderstanding caused by this commitment to others not so dedicated; metanoia — a changing of one's life; inner healing; meditation; purification; the stripping away of inessentials; self-sacrifice.

XIII the washer at the ford

XIII   The Washer at the Ford

Description: At a ford by night, the Washer at the Ford washes bloody linen. A raven perches upon a boundary stone, while in the distance hounds bay under a gibbous moon.

Background: The Washer at the Ford is one of the oldest figures of death in Celtic tradition. Those who see her washing out bloody linen are normally warriors whose vision of her presages their pending death in battle.

The north-west European tradition is at variance with Classical tradition in depicting a woman as the archetype of death, but this is the dark face of the Goddess who though she gives birth to all creation, gathers it all back at the end of time. The Valkyries of Norse legend, the choosers of the slain, are not so very different from the threefold Goddess, the Morrighan, who, under her personas of Badb, Macha and Nemainn, pick the battlefield clean in the form of ravens. Breton tradition also has its *Lavendiers de la Nuit* — women who haunt streams at midnight, washing linen.[19] The woman ('the Nightmare-Life-in-Death') who dices with death in Coleridge's *The Rime of the Ancient Mariner* draws on this very same tradition.

The Washer at the Ford is one of the aspects of Morgan, who

inherits the mythos attached to the Morrighan. Geoffrey of Monmouth describes her as 'Morgen, a Goddess, who receives Arthur into her island realm of Avalon, there to heal him of his wounds'.[9] Later texts make Morgan a mortal woman but a powerful enchanter, bent on bringing Arthur to his ruin: this development shows a fusion of early traditions and results in a character who is indeed aligned to the Morrighan of Irish myth.

Elsewhere, in oral Welsh tradition, she is called Modron, the Great Mother. It is she who is encountered by Urien of Rheged at the Ford of Barking; by him she conceives twin children, Owain and Morfydd. (This Owain features in 'The Dream of Rhonabwy' and other romances of the *Mabinogion* both as Arthur's champion and his opponent.) Urien does not die in this story, for his encounter with Modron results in a birth, not a death.[41] Modron is the mother of Mabon (see p.56) and her search for him is comparable to Ceridwen's pursuit of Taliesin (see p.31.): both women depict the archetype of the Goddess as initiator.

The Washer at the Ford is essentially a challenging figure, yet she is also known as the Dark Woman of Knowledge in tradition because she is a teacher who initiates us into knowledge of ourselves.

Archetypal Meaning: The Washer at the Ford is the shape-changer, challenging and inviting all who approach her to change. She represents renewal, changing that which is static into that which is vital. Her katabolic action destroys outworn ideas, leaving room for fresh growth. Hers is a positive destruction, a clearing away of old growths.

Divinatory Meaning: The elimination of outworn ideas, stale relationships and static customs; fallowness; sexual union; ecstasy; the disruption of old patterns; renewal; ruthless yet compassionate action.

XIV   The Cauldron

Description: In an underworld cavern hangs the cauldron of

xno the cauldron

rebirth, tended by three women: a maiden, a woman and a crone. The carvings behind them depict ancient kings, including Pen Annwn, the Lord of the Underworld. Near the cauldron an adder darts.

Background: The cauldron is the main object of Arthur's descent into Annwn on the ship Prydwen. The poem *Preiddeu Annwn*[29] tells that the cauldron owned by Pen Annwn is cooled by the breath of nine maidens. This card depicts three figures tending the cauldron, for the ninefold sisterhood referred to in the poem are really aspects of the Goddess who frequently appears under three guises.[41] Such a sisterhood are under the aegis of Morgen in the Vita Merlini,[9] where they are said to be in possession of the arts and sciences. Morgen herself is a healer in this text, and various parallel texts speak of her ability with the admixture and brewing of herbal remedies for the care of Arthur's wounds.

We are already familiar with the story of Taliesin and Ceridwen's cauldron which is one of knowledge and inspiration (see p.31), as well as with the cauldron of rebirth which Bran the Blessed owns. The cauldron which Arthur seeks is said to be one which will not boil the food of a coward. This vessel clearly reflects the Celtic custom of apportioning special cuts of meat for warriors, poets, kings etc., all of which we laid down by law. Some aspect of all three cauldrons is apparent in the vessel of the Grail itself, for it gives knowledge of the Otherworld, it renews the Wasteland and heals the Wounded King, and it gives the food which everyone desires, according to various sources. [31]

The chains by which the cauldron hangs in this card connect the three worlds: the Underworld, here represented by the ancient kings, the ancestral heroes who have descended to seek the wisdom of the cauldron; the Earth, which seeks the empowerment of the cauldron; and the Otherworld, represented by the sisterhood tending the cauldron. Both ancestral kings and maidens oversee the regenerative forces of the cauldron; they are the Sons of Knowledge and Daughters of Memory within Celtic tradition — a concept also known as the interrelation of the sibyls and prophets in later Christian tradition. [38]

Archetypal Meaning: The Cauldron represents the regeneration of all orders of creation in the land of Logres. There is no loss, only changing and transmutation in this life beyond life. It is the source of spiritual empowerment to the initiate who goes beyond the gates of death in the search for the Grail.

Divinatory Meaning: Regeneration; fusion; recombination of resources or potentials; tempering outer circumstance by inner values; blending or merging with a new idea; polarized living; correct balancing of one's personality.

XV The Green Knight

Description: The Green Knight stands in the entrance of a hall. The winter snow swirls in with him. He carries a great axe and is dressed in evergreen leaves. A wren sits by the door.

Background: The famous entrance of the Green Knight into Arthur's Christmas court is recorded in the fourteenth-century text, *Sir Gawain and the Green Knight* [18] but the story has much earlier analogues. The Green Knight bursts into the

xo the green knight

hall bringing a winter game or challenge called the Beheading Game. He offers his axe to any challenger, kneeling so that his head can be cut off: in return the challenger must also kneel and offer his head to the axe. No one imagines that the return blow will ever be struck, and only Gawain takes up the challenge. After he has cut off the Green Knight's head, the Green Knight rises and demands that Gawain meet him a year hence and offer his head to the Beheading Game. Gawain eventually meets his opponent, after sojourning at the house of Sir Bertilak, at the Green Chapel. He kneels for the blow, but is only nicked on the neck with the blade of the axe, since he was tempted by Betilak's wife into accepting magical assistance of a green garter against his opponent. It transpires that the Green Knight is none other than his host, Sir Bertilak. Arthur decrees thereafter that Gawain shall employ the green garter as his emblem, in token of his challenge.

The prime forerunner of this story is told in the Ulster cycle where Cuchulainn is similarly challenged by a terrible giant who is Cu Roi mac Daire, King of Munster, in disguise. In this version, three warriors take up the giant's challenge, but only Cuchulainn is brave enough to face the return blow and it is he who is accorded praise as the Champion of Ulster and given the hero's portion of the feast.[5] The fact that we have both early and later versions of the same story means that we can observe the nature of Gawain's role as Champion of Britain.

The medieval story explains away the mystery of the Green Knight by making him an ordinary knight, Sir Bertilak, who has been placed under enchantment by Morgan le Fay. In the earlier version, we see that Cu Roi mac Daire is a powerful Otherworldly figure in his own right, well able to test and try the warriors of Ulster. He has been identified as an instrument of the Goddess of Sovereignty, and so the part of Morgan in the later story also becomes clear: for Morgan is herself a manifestation of the Goddess in her aspect of Cailleach or Dark Woman of Knowledge. Behind both the Green Knight and Morgan we can discern a pair or archetypes: the Lord and Lady of the Wheel, who stand as guardians and challengers within the Spiral Tower. [41]

The Beheading Game incorporates an ancient tradition concerning the King of Winter and the King of Summer, sometimes polarized as the kings of the Otherworld and of Britain. Gawain's earlier name, Gwalchmai, Hawk of May, indicates that he is the candidate for the King of Summer or Britain. Tradition also makes him stronger as the sun reaches midday. The Green Knight, attired in midwinter evergreen, is the King of Winter or the Otherworld, and he stands for the old year which cedes place to the new year, in the person of Gawain. The wren which roosts at the Green Knight's feet is symbolic of the sacrificial bird. It is still processed in parts of Ireland in a folk custom enacted by the Wren Boys who sing:

The wren, the wren, the king of all birds,
On St Stephen's day was lost in the furze.
Although he is little, his portion is great . . . [54]

Archetypal Meaning: The Green Knight represents the challenger whom all seekers meet on their quest. He answers questions and gives advice, but he also sets riddles and puzzles. Those who think that they know everything he leads astray and torments. His greatest desire is to be bested by a worthy opponent.

Divinatory Meaning: Challenge; obstacles which must be overcome; ignorance; self-limitation; inflexibility; unconscious fears realized; stagnation; incisive change; creative possibilities.

XVI   The Spiral Tower

Description: Upon a high tor, a tower is struck by lightning, masonry falls to the ground. But while the physical tower is shattered, a spiral tower of crystal remains. About the tor, the signs of the zodiac glow within the land. An owl flies upwards.

Background: Throughout the search for the Grail, the questers encounter many dangers and tests. Only one seeker is destined to find the regenerating vessel in each age, although it is a quest which all seekers are directed to follow individually. The Grail finder in the Arthurian legends is Perceval or Peredur in the earliest texts. Later tradition gives this task to Galahad, Lancelot's son; his two companions are Perceval and Bors.[31]

The Grail is only achieved by the worthiest quester, just as Sovereignty only accepts the worthiest candidate for the kingship of the land. When it is achieved, the Grail passes out of manifestation as a symbolic cup and becomes imprinted

xvi the spiral tower

physically in the life of the land and its peoples.

This cycle of change is seldom appreciated, being viewed as a catastrophic alteration of the patterns of time and space. This is apparent in the later Arthurian cycle where the achieving of the Grail heralds the breaking of the Round Table Fellowship. But though the Round Table knights meet no more, the concept of the fellowship remains etched in the land itself.

The Grail is withdrawn in order that its influence shall become operative and remain so. The Grail winner also becomes withdrawn or dead to the world, in some sense. Sometimes his physical body seems to die, as Galahad does at Sarras upon looking in the Grail itself.[31] In other traditions, it is Perceval who wins the Grail; he remains in the Otherworld or on the borders of this world and the other, in order to mediate between the land and its peoples, becoming the new Grail King. In reality the Grail winner lives a life beyond life. His physical body is the vehicle for earthly existence only. By his achievement he or she is changed, transfigured to partake of both existences, mediating the regenerative influence of the Grail to all seekers.

Glastonbury has traditionally been associated with the Grail and Arthur, almost from the beginning of the tradition. It is a special place of pilgrimage which veils a deeper reality. The physical contours of the land are aligned to inner potencies that can be contacted at different times of the year. It is perhaps for this reason that it has been called 'this holiest earth'. There is no physical earth zodiac at Glastonbury: this is a transcendent reality mediated by the Grail guardian whose point of contact is the Tor itself: a locus which is mystical and actual at once.[32] The shattering of the Round Table on earth sees its reformation in the Otherworld. The Spiral Tower is the place of initiation within Celtic tradition. Each individual has a different experience therein. But only a poet like Taliesin is enabled to speak, however obscurely, about what one finds there.

Archetypal Meaning: The Spiral Tower represents the inner hostel of all seekers, where spiritual nourishment is given and deep instruction imparted. Within Logres, it functions as the spiral pathway to the Glass Caer of a new existence. Within its confines the current Grail guardian of the epoch will be found.

Divinatory Meaning: Reversal of energies; withdrawal of old customs, phases and concepts; shocking change; liberation from outworn concepts; humility; the realization of limitations; natural forces at work; a curative illness, e.g. one which expels poisons from the body; loss of cosy security; transfiguration; self-awareness.

XVII   The Star

Description: A hill-fort at night. Two watchmen, one asleep, are witness to the dragon-shaped comet which rushes across the sky, breaking through the constellation of Great Bear. From its mouth stream two rays of light. A cockerel proclaims the hope which is to come, although it is not yet dawn.

Background: In his *History of the Kings of Britain*, Geoffrey of Monmouth writes about a meteor in dragon shape which appeared over Logres. Uther called Merlin to interpret this omen. Merlin immediately announced the death of Ambrosius Aurelianus, and urged Uther to become King of

xvii the star

Britain. The dragon was interpreted as being Uther himself and the two rays which came from the dragon's mouth signified his son, Arthur, whose dominion would be great, and Uther's daughter, Anna, whose sons and grandsons would be kings of Britain. Uther immediately ordered the making of two golden dragons, one of which he gave to the cathedral of Winchester and the other of which he carried into battle.[8]

The dragon-star then heralds the coming of the Pendragons, and the golden dragon which Uther has made is the draco standard which is carried into battle as a sign of hope and victory.

Throughout the history of Logres, the hope of the people is ever renewed as the tides of time ebb and flow. At the conclusion of Arthur's reign, when all seems in despair, hope rises of a new coming which is both resurrection and a new birth at once. When all seems dark, the duty of the seeker is to look ever for signs of renewal, to be vigilant at all times, to encourage the down-hearted and strengthen the doubtful.

Just as the land of Logres was in disarray before the coming of the Pendragons, so all times of crisis need their inspiration and rallying point. Here the vulnerability of the land finds a new protector, announced by a heavenly sign. As the Grail guardian is withdrawn into the Spiral Tower, so a new cycle is imminent.

In every land, in every time, there are guardians who were once seekers. Like Merlin, they read the signs of the times and wait in order to help the influence of the Otherworld to manifest. In every land and every time, individuals whose vocation is to bring great change or greater cohesion are being born. The precession of the equinoxes which brings us into the New Age, reveals many such people, and they are our hope.

Archetypal Meaning: The Star of Prophecy represents the springs of hope in the land of Logres. The seeker is bidden to be watchful and faithful in his or her service, ready to sublimate his or her energies to all manifestations of justice, truth and integrity.

Divinatory Meaning: Hope; renewal; the beginning of a new cycle; inspiration; faith born of desire and trust; love of another's good; refreshment; the raising of popular consciousness.

XVIII   The Moon

Description: Under a full moon stand two dark towers. The moon encloses an embryonic child, curled as though in the womb. Striving to leap the weir is a solitary salmon.

Background: There is always a period of waiting before the Pendragon or the Grail winner show themselves to the people. In the case of Arthur, he is taken from his parents, Igraine and Uther, by Merlin to a place of fosterage where he will learn the skills which he will need when he is king. Perceval is raised in the seclusion of a forest, in ignorance of arms and knighthood, by his mother.[4] Galahad is raised in a monastery.[31] Lancelot is fostered by the Lady of the Lake and taught the skills of war as well as the courtly manners of a noble youth. Nothing can hasten this necessary process of preparation any more than a child in the womb can be born before the time is right.

The coming of Arthur and the Grail champions stand in the

xviii the moon

long tradition of the Wondrous Youth who is destined to reappear after a period of devastation or despair. Within Celtic tradition this youth is called Mabon, the son of Modron. These names mean, respectively, Son and Mother, and they represent archetypes which can be identified and reapplied to many of the figures within the Arthurian tradition.

Mabon's story survives fragmentedly in 'Culhwch and Olwen' in the *Mabinogion*, [30] where he becomes the object of a quest by Culhwch, a youth who is set many impossible tasks in order to win his chosen bride, Olwen, the giant's daughter. Arthur and his court assist Culhwch in accomplishing his tasks.

Culhwch is told to find Mabon, a mysterious character who was taken 'from between his mother and the wall when he was three nights old and no-one knows whether he is alive or dead'. By questing through the levels of time, each represented by a totemic bird, beast or fish, Culhwch and his companions are enabled to find the Salmon, the oldest of the animals in Celtic tradition — who takes them to Mabon's place of imprisonment. There he is liberated, no longer a baby, but a vigorous youth who is both harpist and hunter. Mabon further assists Culhwch achieve his tasks. [44]

In this fragmentary mystery story, Mabon's imprisonment is not necessarily an unwilling one. Just as the Grail passes out of manifestation into a withdrawn state, so too do certain archetypes wait for the right moment before manifesting again. Mabon's imprisonment is hinted at in the *Preiddeu Annwn* [9] where he is described as a youth bound with golden fetters — a hostage to the Otherworld who awaits from the beginning of time for a chance to manifest.

Mabon's story is clearly paralleled by that of Taliesin who, as Gwion Bach, was transformed as an initiate poet-seer into many forms, including the salmon who, as the oldest of animals, taught him all wisdom. He suffered 'three periods in the prison of Arianrhod': a reference to the Spiral or Glass Caer of initiation. Lastly he was born of Ceridwen, his instructor in wisdom.

Mabon is the son of his mother, the Goddess Modron, but

his father is not mentioned in any tradition. This aligns him with Merlin who is likewise 'a child without a father'.

Archetypal Meaning: The Moon represents the inner destiny of the One Who Will Come, be he or she monarch, hero, poet, seer or champion of truth. The potentiality of Logres strives to be born in this card, but it remains latent until the times and tides are right for it to manifest.

Divinatory Meaning: Clear visualization; generation; cyclic patterns of growth; fertility and increase; fluctuation; dreams and visions; introspection; necessary preparation; fallowness; the seasonal round; the tides of time.

XIX   The Sun

Description: Under the midday sun rides a naked youth upon a white mare. On his back is a harp; in his hand a spear.

Background: In the card of the Moon, we saw the embryonic child growing in the womb of the Goddess. In this card, Mabon emerges into the world, ready to set out on his quest. As stated in the previous entry, Mabon's role is an archetypal one which can be applied to more than one of the Arthurian heroes. The

xix the sun

youthful hero whose innocence and worthiness shine from him usually comes into a world torn by war and confusion. In his aspect of innocent youth, the hero brings a new perspective and the wisdom of his mother.

Mabon's mother, Modron, is here represented by the white mare on which he rides. The White Mare was emblematic of the sovereignty of the Goddess, frequently appearing as a chalk hill figure or on Celtic coins. (The same image may be found on Arthur's throne in card IV.) The White Mare was how the Celtic Goddess, Epona, was represented. She, Macha and Rhiannon share a common symbology. [44]

Throughout Celtic tradition, we read of youthful heroes who vindicate their mothers in some way or else they become champions of their land. Usually their mothers are disgraced or sent into slavery. In order to preserve the life of their sons, these women send their children into fosterage where they obtain the necessary empowerment to return and overthrow an oppressive king or stepfather.

Arthur's career begins when he successfully pulls the sword from the stone. This is not the same sword as Excalibur in later legend, for that is gifted him by the Lady of the Lake and is one of the Hallows. The ability to pull the sword from the stone is a sovereignty-bestowing act and Arthur becomes king, bringing his youthful might to restore the kingdom.

The archetype of Mabon derives from the Romano-British god, Maponus, who was very popular among the legionaries along Hadrian's Wall, as well as among the tribes of the north. The Romans incorporated many Classical features into this archetype, chief of which are those of Apollo. Whether earlier, Druidic teachings had already made this connection cannot be proved, but the overlay is certainly there. Mabon, like Apollo, is both harpist and hunter. In both roles, the God is searchingly direct: he meets injustice either by the challenge of his judgement, represented by his harp — for he is judge, poet and Druid — or else by force of arms.

In Arthurian tradition, we find the twofold role is represented by different sorts of men: the knights, such as

Perceval, Gawain and Kay, exercise their chivalric skills in defence of their land; the poet-seers, such as Taliesin and Merlin, bring the clarity of their prophetic and poetic insight so that injustice is brought out and exposed publicly.

It is only Arthur himself and Mabon who still combine both roles within them.

Archetypal Meaning: The Sun represents the outer or revealed destiny of the One Who Will Come, be he or she monarch, poet, seer, hero or champion of truth. The Sun conquers by innocence, revealing falsehood by its shining beams, and gladdening the earth with its warmth.

Divinatory Meaning: Innocence; purity; enthusiasm; warmth; a loving heart; joy, freedom; enlightenment; wholeness; health; intolerance of shadows in any aspect of life; clarity; directness; true vocation realized.

XX   The Sleeping Lord

Description: The gigantic figure of the Sleeping Lord lies as a hill, incorporated into the land itself. On his thigh stands the youthful hero blowing a horn. All about the landscape, people of many kinds, ages and eras rise out of their tombs and

xx the sleeping lord

barrows. They look upwards to a great eagle which flies overhead.

Background: Consistent within Arthurian tradition is the assertion that Arthur will come again. Many hills and sites have been associated with this legend, and stories have been told about daring individuals who entered the Hollow Hills to discover Arthur and his court asleep therein. Usually the finder is given the opportunity to summon Arthur from sleep by blowing a horn, drawing the sword from its scabbard, or cutting the baldric which lies near the king. But though he is tempted to do so, the finder usually returns to his own world without doing this, because Arthur may only be awakened in the time of Britain's greatest need.

The medieval poet, Lydgate, wrote of Arthur:

> *He is King crouned in Fairie,*
> *With Sceptre and sword and with his regally*
> *Shall resort as Lord and Soveraigne*
> *Out of Fairie and reigne in Britaine;*
> *And repaire again the Round Table.*
> *By prophesy Merlin set the date*
> *Among princes King incomparable,*
> *His seat again to Caerlion to translate,*
> *The Parchas sustren sponne so his fate,*
> *His epitaph recordeth so certaine,*
> *Here lieth King Arthur that shall raigne again.* [30]

The undying legend of Arthur is like this very same story of regeneration and perpetual defence of the land, a role which has been applied to many military leaders, monarchs and heroes who throughout the history of Britain have attracted similar legends.

The sleep of the Pendragon beneath the land or in Avalon is very like the burial of Bran the Blessed's head under the White Mount: both kings are Palladiums of their country. And yet no one character can be expected to remain in this condition forever. New guardians and protectors continually emerge: they are born, they fulfil their vocations and they pass again into the renewal of the Otherworld. Within the context of the inner sovereignty of the land, a cycle which has been identified as the Succession of the Pendragons is discernible.[44] This is not a familial or necessarily royal lineage, but an initiatic one which is open to all seekers.

The return of Arthur is a prophesied event which can happen at the changing of the tides of time, at the turning of the aeons. It can happen, has happened and will happen within the circles of eternity. Time is not what we have understood it to be and the ways of regeneration are wonderful and mysterious to us.

Archetypal Meaning: The Sleeping Lord represents abiding promise of renewal. He indicates the apocatastasis — the point where creation is drawn back to its origins and remade. When Arthur or any salvific figure comes again, the times are understood to be at their end and their beginning. Those who partake of the mysteries are liberated from time into an unknown existence governed by the Dwellers in Avalon.

Divinatory Meaning: Renewal, resurrection; recapitulation of events or ideas; prophetic vision; ending or beginning; forgiveness; adjustment; recovery of that which has been lost sight of; impulse to change one's life.

XXI The Flowering of Logres

Description: In a burgeoning landscape, the Seeker dances with two children. The rainbow scarf which is held in their hands swirls out to border the scene. Beyond and around it is the starry firmament in which the liberated and active Hallows of the land, the Sword, Spear, Grail and Stone, are illuminated.

Background: The restoration of the Wasteland is the hope and goal of the Seeker. This can be achieved by the quest for the Hallows and by their skilful wielding in the world. When the land is restored, the Wounded King is healed, a new Grail guardian is appointed and Sovereignty assumes her beautiful

guise as the Maiden Goddess.

This search for the Hallows happens at many levels of existence: their finding correspondingly has many ripples throughout creation. All peoples, animals and growing things are brought into contact with the deep springs which well up as a result of the empowered Hallows.

The Seeker in card XXI is a different person from the quester who set out in card 0. He has undergone a severe and testing journey. The two children with whom he dances in joyful celebration are the same two who appeared in card V, listening to Taliesin's story. These archetypal children are the twin innocents whose dwelling is the terrestial paradise. Within the Grail texts, they appear to Perceval and guide him on his journey.[58] The links of tradition lie in their hands, ready to pass on to other seekers in other ages. The rainbow road upon which the Seeker set out has become a woven scarf which encompasses the world.

The Hallowquest is not a selfish or individual regeneration, for the healing of one person, their alignment with their true spiritual source, is also the partial healing of the land. The healing of one land is a partial healing of the world. There is still a great deal of work to be done. May your own quest be fruitful!

Archetypal Meaning: The Flowering of Logres represents the restoration of fertility on all levels. The moment of renewal announces a timeless joy throughout the hearts of all orders of creation: rocks, plants, animals and people. The quest is over for one cycle. There will be other seekers and other quests.

Divinatory Meaning: Restoration; culmination; triumph, attainment; perfection; rapture; spiritual healing; creative growth; the new aeon.

THE LESSER POWERS

The following section gives descriptions and divinatory meanings for the Lesser Powers. The backgrounds which accompany these cards suggest ways in which each card can be further explored. They are not essential to an understanding of the *Hallowquest* Tarot, although they may act as useful information and further reading if you wish to use the cards for story-telling or if you employ the Three Worlds Spread (see p.133).Some of the stories referred to here are to be found in fuller form in *Hallowquest: Tarot Magic and the Arthurian Mysteries*, but due to lack of space the reader is referred to the bibliography. The stories are drawn from the widest possible frame of reference, including both the early British and later French romances.

Sword: Air, Spring

Sword Hallow
Description: Out of a dark underground chamber arises hot steam. The Sword of Light rises up in scintillating brilliance.

Background: The ancient Glaive or Sword of Light which is wielded by the hero in Celtic folk story is the prototype of this Hallow, as is the Sword of Nuadu in Irish tradition.

Meaning: Incisive energy; the dispelling of illusions; conquest;

championship; strength and power; love of truth and justice; the power of the mind; rational deduction or perception; light in dark places.

Sword Two
Description: Under a hazy sun is a steep wooded valley with a path running through it. On either side of the path two swords are stuck into the earth. An adder darts from the grass.

Background: The Battle of Camlan, sometimes called the last battle within the Arthurian legends, is suggested in this card; the two swords represent the armies of Arthur and Mordred drawn up in truce. An adder moving in the grass caused a man to draw his sword to slay it, and so battle was provoked.[41]

Meaning: Amnesty or temporary peace; indecision; compromise; suspension of deeply-held beliefs or opinions; hesitation; analysis of the situation is required before action.

Sword Three
Description: A gorge in mountainous country with a broken bridge. A sword falls into the gorge.

Background: When Peredur or Perceval left his mother, she died of sorrow. But this was as a direct result of her

sword three   sword four

possessiveness, which caused her to raise her son in ignorance of weapons and the way of knighthood in the seclusion of the forest. Perceval would have been unable and unprepared to achieve the Grail had he stayed at home. [4]

Meaning: Sorrow; separation; deep disappointment; loss; the possession of the thoughts by jealousy; brooding upon personal slights; it is necessary to analyse one's receptivity to the tide of events and acknowledge one's responsibility for others' pain.

Sword Four
Description: A sword lies on the altar within a chapel or hermitage.

Background: Although Perceval learns skill at arms from his uncle, his education is incomplete until he learns from his other, hermit uncle, the ways of the spirit. Traditionally, novice knights laid their swords on the altar before taking their final chivalric vows.

Meaning: Respite; hermetic seclusion; meditation; self-exile or retreat; convalescence; rest; replenishment of spirit; solitude; it is time to reassess one's powers and limitations in quiet seclusion.

Sword Five

Description: Heathland swept by war and destruction. Beside a burning house, a broken sword lies.

Background: Throughout the Arthurian legends, we encounter many criminal knights, none more so than Sir Bruce Sans Pitié, whose cruelty and devious methods make him an enemy to be feared. He is finally overcome by Lancelot, but not before he has caused widespread suffering and destruction. [31]

Meaning: Defeat; slander; cowardice; unethical behaviour; divisive means; thwarted plans; sloppy or malicious thinking causes things to go awry.

Sword Six

Description: A quiet sunny river winds through a willow copse. A sword stands in a barge which is moored nearby.

Background: After the many trials and difficulties of the Grail knights, a ship appears mysteriously to bear Galahad, Bors, Perceval and Dindraine further upon their quest. [36]

Meaning: Success after trouble; safety and protection; a journey; new perspectives; difficulties and blockages are cleared as a result of perceptive thought.

Sword Seven

Description: A river in full flood. A stone floats in the waters with a sword stuck into it.

Background: When Galahad first comes to Arthur's court, he is summoned to the Adventure of the Stone. This consists of a floating red stone in which a sword is stuck. Many of Arthur's knights are totally unable to pull it forth, but Galahad succeeds, thus emulating Arthur, who came to the throne by pulling a sword from a stone.[31]

Meaning: Unstable effort; little progress; plans fail as a result of confused thinking; self-deceit; passivity; over-defensiveness; the need for proper conceptualization.

Sword Eight

Description: In a brown marsh, a sword stands solitary.

Background: Gereint's stubborn attempt to prove himself a man of prowess in Enid's eyes leads him into many fruitless adventures in which he is wounded. His own pride forbids him to ask Arthur's help and he exiles himself from court in a further series of mad adventures.[30]

Meaning: Restriction; one's bounden duty; fear of what others say; bigoted opinions; intolerance; imprisonment;

illness; thinking is in bondage; the time for out-worn thought patterns is over.

Sword Nine

Description: Night. Under a waning moon is a palisaded fence with severed heads upon its spikes. In a ditch lies a sword.

Background: The culmination of Gereint's self-determined quest for knightly accolade leads him to the court of Owain where the Enchanted Games are held. This challenge consists of entering a magical enclosure, surrounded by a palisaded fence on which the heads of former challengers are staked. [30]

Meaning: Suffering; grave doubts; guilt; premonitions and nightmares; cruelty; despair; depression; inability to take personal responsibility for one's path; the need for a disciplined life-style and commitment to logical thought.

Sword Ten

Description: A fortified lake dwelling is reached only by a narrow stone bridge. On the near bank stands a sword, while over the bridge a hawk hovers in the rain.

Background: When Guinevere is abducted by Meleagrance and held captive in his castle, Lancelot comes to the rescue.

sword nine

sword ten

The only means of entry is by means of a perilously narrow sword bridge over which Lancelot crawls in order to rescue the queen.[4]

Meaning: Life and death decision; the final solution dictated by ruthless logic; pain; affliction; total oppression; masochism; the need for extreme daring and resolution; the acknowledgement and confrontation of karmic debts.

Sword Maiden

Description: Under a tree sits the Sword Maiden embroidering a scabbard. She has cut off her own hair to make a plaited belt for the sword.

Background: Dindraine, Perceval's sister, is part of the Grail quest. She cuts off her hair in order to weave a belt for the sword which Galahad shall carry.[36]

Meaning: She quickly grasps ideas and materializes them; perceptive and discerning, she is vigilant in the cause of truth and justice; she cuts through difficulties by taking the way of self-sacrifice.

Sword Knight

Description: At dawn, the Sword Knight rides on a dun horse, raising his sword to the distant tower.

sword maiden

sword knight

Background: It is Llwch Lleawc or Lleminawc the Irishman who, in the *Preiddeu Annwn* wields the Sword of Light and enables Arthur to steal the cauldron of Pen Annwn. This character's name and attributes are reflected in the person of the later Lancelot.[44]

Meaning: He is incisive and fearless, prompt to defend the weak and swift to halt injustice; he asserts the idea of right with skill and courage; he is the upholder of the Sword of Light.

Sword Queen

Description: The Sword Queen sits on a fallen tree burnishing a sword.

Background: The Black Maiden who admonishes Perceval for not persevering in his quest and for not asking the all-important Grail question well represents the Sword Queen. In *Peredur*, part of her role is fulfilled by one of the Nine Witches of Gloucester who train Peredur in arms, after the fashion of Celtic warrior women.[30]

Meaning: She is intelligent and self-reliant, speaking her mind and not suffering fools gladly; as the defender of the unprotected, she is assiduous and fair-minded; she imparts a sense of justice to all who encounter her.

Sword King

Description: The Sword King sits enthroned with his sword, on the mound of justice.

Background: The medieval romances made Arthur the paragon of justice and law-giving. The Round Table Fellowship was founded in the spirit of justice for all and for protection of the weak. From it Arthur dispensed the laws that made his kingdom great. [31]

Meaning: He is the giver of justice, a wise counsellor whose analytical judgements cut right to the heart of the matter; his severity is tempered by impartiality and he shows how self-analysis and love of truth may govern one's life.

Spear: Fire, Summer

Spear Hallow

Description: From deep cracks in the earth, sheets of fire flame up. The Spear which both heals and wounds rises up with great force and power.

Background: The Spear which heals and wounds is the prime implement which both causes and heals the Wasteland, depending upon who wields it. When it is touched to the Wounded King's wounds, health enters both king and land. [79]

Meaning: Creativity; the beginning of a project; innovation; purpose; birth; the faculty of intuition; inspiration; energy; challenge; the healing of all that is corrupt.

Spear Two

Description: On a hillside overlooking a network of fields is a sparrowhawk on a perch. A spear stands beside the path which leads into the valley.

Background: In order to avenge Guinevere, Gereint pursues the knight who insulted her. He enters the Sparrowhawk Contest in which he overcomes the knight and wins the game. [30]

Meaning: Choice; control; mastery; the skilled organization of resources leads to achievement of desire; intuitive synthesis; dynamic drive.

Spear Three

Description: The path leads between the trees in a beechwood. A spear points the way.

Background: During the Quest the knights often met with guidance through the vast entanglement of the Forests of Adventure. Sometimes this took the form of a hermit figure, sometimes of two naked children sitting in a tree and indicating the way.[58]

Meaning: Established strength; controlled intention; intuitive understanding gives an expansive outlook and resulting opportunities; scrupulous responsibility; enterprising initiative.

Spear Four

Description: The path leads from distant woods, branching off at a settlement. Beside the path stands a garlanded spear.

Background: After Gereint succeeded in the Enchanted Games, the Joy of the Court was celebrated. This relates closely to the central mystery of the *Hallowquest*.[41]

Meaning: Completion of an enterprise; a time of festival and celebration; enjoyment of the fruits of one's labours; harmonious conclusion; acknowledgement of intuitive strength.

Spear Five
Description: Against a setting sun are crossed spears against a monolith.

Background: The combat of Balin and Balan is the most

grievous in the whole of Arthurian literature, since they are brothers and they kill each other, unknowingly. Balin's sword is set by Merlin in a floating stone which Galahad later draws to prove his right to sit at the Round Table. [31]

Meaning: Contention and strife; salutary struggle; competitiveness; dictatorial attitudes cause obstruction; the need to distinguish between rightful intuition and unassuaged desires.

Spear Six
Description: Beside a winding river is a ceremonial mound on which sticks a spear with a standard of victory on it.

Background: At the beginning of his reign Arthur success-fully defeated 11 kings who were opposed to his rule. He then went on to conquer Scandinavia and Gaul, approaching the very gates of Rome itself. [8]

Meaning: Victory; advancement realized through steady growth; pride in achievement; recognition; intuitively self-confident; ceremonial honours.

Spear Seven
Description: At the entrance to a stone fort, a spear stands, defensively.

Background: The historical figure of Arthur successfully united the Romano-British forces to defeat the invading Saxons, thus turning conquest into settlement and earning himself an honoured place in history. [46]

Meaning: Courageous ability; success despite opposition; tenacity and persistence upheld by strong intuition; defence of strongly-held beliefs.

Spear Eight
Description: A mountain river in spate takes a spear downstream.

Background: Tristan and Isolt frequently saved themselves

from capture by King Mark by the expedient of twigs floating downriver on which were carved secret signs as a means of warning.[31]

Meaning: Swiftness; expediency; hasty perpetration of intuitions; prophetic insight; speedy progress and rapid growth; communication.

Spear Nine
Description: A turbulent sea crashes against high, jagged cliffs, on which a spear stands.

Background: Woken from sleep Arthur spied a strange ship in which was the body of a dead knight. He learned from the letter in the knight's hand of the mysterious events surrounding the Grail.[3]

Meaning: Enduring strength; great reserves; dedication to intuitive purpose; obstinacy; defensiveness; the wisdom to prepare against adversity.

Spear Ten
Description: The path leads down into a valley and climbs to a distant hill-fort. Beside the path stands the spear. Two ravens guard the way.

Background: Corbin or Corbinec was the home of the Grail King, Pelles. He was wounded in both thighs and unable to walk, and awaited the coming of the Grail winner to heal him.[31]

Meaning: Responsibility; excessive burdens; over-expansion of resources; resolution by test of fire; crisis brings restoration; the need to delegate to others or the readjustment of power in order that the intuitive faculties can operate.

Spear Maiden

Description: The Spear Maiden runs with her spear raised. On her right wrist is a hawk.

Background: Lunet or Linnet is the resourceful maiden who guides Owain or Gareth to help her mistress. She gives Owain a ring of invisibility and helps him avoid capture.[4, 30]

Meaning: She is a resourceful and enthusiastic messenger, faithful and loyal, if uninhibited and forthright; she shows the way through impossible situations by her daring, often by disguise or shape-shifting.

Spear Knight

Description: Under the midday sun, the Spear Knight rides full pelt on a roan horse, with spear raised.

spear maiden

spear knight

Background: Bedwyr is one of Arthur's chief warrior companions in the early texts. It is said of his spear that the head of the shaft would leave the lance and draw blood from the wind before returning to its shaft again. He aids Culhwch in many adventures. [30]

Meaning: He is an energetic and impetuous champion; his inspired companionship leads into exciting adventures; but he is fearless of the unknown and his hasty decisions are often risky.

spear queen

spear king

Spear Queen

Description: The Spear Queen offers her spear, kneeling in front of a number of grave mounds. The spear drips with blood.

Background: The Lady of the Fountain's husband is killed by Owain in a magical contest of arms. Afterwards, Owain marries the Lady with Lunet's encouragement and help, and so the Lady's lands are held against her enemies once more. But before she can be persuaded to take Owain, she mourns her husband grieviously. [30]

Meaning: She is deeply attuned to the needs of the land and has suffered in its service; her grief is well hidden and she is generous and friendly to all; she imparts a deep commitment to the healing of the earth.

Spear King

Description: At a forge, the Spear King tests the keenness of his spear's point.

Background: Perceval's uncle, as part of his initiatory training, demands that he sever an iron staple which immediately renews itself after each blow. [4]

Meaning: He is honest and passionate, committed to his intuitive understanding of the land, even to the point of sacrifice; he teaches the ways of healing by his wisdom; he is the upholder of the Spear which both heals and wounds.

Grail: Water, Autumn

Grail Hallow

Description: Out of the living rock, a swift underground stream rushes in a great fall. The Grail appears in refulgent light.

Background: The Grail is prefigured in many proto-Celtic stories of cauldrons and enchanted vessels. It gives fulfilment, fertility and joy. [52]

gRail hallow

gRail two

Meaning: Fertility; abundance; nurture; spiritual joy; healing; gladness; the emotional faculty; restoration after barrenness.

Grail Two

Description: In autumn elm woods, two doves drink from an earthenware dish.

Background: The dove is one of the prime totems of the Grail. It appears on the head-dress of the Grail messenger, Kundrie. When the Grail knights see this, they rejoice for they recognize that the achieving of the Grail is not far off.[79]

Meaning: Love; harmony; partnership; co-operation; concord; emotional reciprocation.

Grail Three

Description: In an apple orchard, a table is set with harvest fare.

Background: One of the prime functions of the Grail is to provide plenty to all who set forth on the Quest. At Camelot, when the Grail first appeared to Arthur and his men, each person received the food he most desired. This can, of course, also means spiritual fare.[31]

Meaning: Abundance; solace, fulfilment; fortunate

grail three

grail four

conclusion; the power to communicate joy and gladness; generosity of spirit.

Grail Four

Description: Near a standing lake of stagnant water, a cup lies overturned in brambles.

Background: It was said of Arthur's kingdom that there were no chalices in all of the land. It was for this reason that many of the knights undertook the Quest for the Grail. [3]

Meaning: Dissatisfaction; lethargy; accidie; stagnation of the spirit; boredom; the need to establish emotional maturity.

Grail Five

Description: A ship with the Grail on its sail makes little headway against swelling seas and heavy mist.

Background: The mysterious Ship of Solomon bore Lancelot to a meeting with his son Galahad. This was a time of great bitterness and disillusion for Lancelot, who learned that he could never achieve the Grail. [36]

Meaning: Disillusion; disappointment; vain regret; the ability to learn from mistakes and assess one's limitations; broken agreements or promises.

grail five

grail six

Grail Six

Description: In a sacred grove of alders, a holy stream rises from a green mound, flowing into a stone basin.

Background: Gawain has his greatest adventure at such a mound, the home of the fearsome Green Knight. From this he learned much and was reconnected with his own past. [18,51]

Meaning: Rediscovery of one's roots; ancestral memories; the pleasure of remembered links; a sense of tradition and continuance; atavism; karmic recall.

grail seven

grail eight

Grail Seven

Description: In the waters of a lake, a fortress is reflected as a faery howe. A cup of silver stands upon the near bank.

Background: When Perceval fails to ask the Grail question, he retires to bed in the Grail castle, but wakes to find the place deserted.[58] Similarly, when Galahad goes to the Castle of Maidens, he is tested. When he refuses to aid the maidens of that place, he discovers that they are not mortal women but enchantments.[31]

Meaning: Self-deception; illusion; an over-active imagination; unrealistic fantasies; the glamour of esoteric practices; the need for emotional discipline.

Grail Eight

Description: Two candles burn on the altar of a chapel while an eight-sided chalice of wine spills upon the floor.

Background: Lancelot reached the very door of the Grail chapel, only to be turned away, blinded and admonished for daring to come so close to the holy object while still living so much in the world.[31]

Meaning: Discontinuance of plans, withdrawal of energies and desire; self-pity; movement away from old beliefs and values; an over-fearful heart; the need to evaluate things from a more universal standpoint.

Grail Nine

Description: Under a starlit sky, a cauldron hangs over a fire.

Background: According to tradition, the Grail provided the food that everyone desired. This stems from the earlier Celtic cauldron stories in which each person at court was accorded a particular cut of the meat boiling within the cauldron.[57]

Meaning: Satisfaction, one's heart's desire; security; physical pleasure; emotional contentment.

Grail Ten

Description: By the seashore, the path leads to a broch. Nearby stands the Grail.

Background: After long and weary search the successful Grail winners arrived at Sarras, the holy place from which all the mysteries of the Grail stemmed. Here they found perfect peace and the contentment of fulfilment.[36]

Meaning: Wholeness; perfection of contentment; fellowship and family; the holiness of the home; peace and happiness; the completion of desire shared by others.

Grail Maiden

Description: Beside a spring, the Grail Maiden stands holding an earthenware vessel.

Background: The Grail Maiden guides all who go in search of the vessel, offering them to drink. Not all recognize the meaning of this gesture, as witness the acts of King Amangons and his men, who raped and despoiled the Damsels of the Wells.[41]

Meaning: She is tender and willing; imaginative and loving, she shows the way to fulfil the deepest desires, often through dreams and visions; she exemplifies the way of service.

grail maiden   grail knight

Grail Knight

Description: The Grail Knight rides upon a white horse through autumn woodlands playing his harp. The Grail appears to him in a beam of sunlight.

Background: The Grail Knight, no matter what his name or origin, always pursues the path to his goal with single-minded truth. An innocent in the ways of the world he is sometimes called 'The Perfect Fool', though his behaviour is never quite what it seems.

Meaning: He is a meditative and poetic champion, often unconventional; his fertile dreams invite fellow travellers to unexplored regions of the quest; he is incorruptible and dedicated.

Grail Queen

Description: Before a rough-hewn doorway in a cliff wall stands the Grail Queen. She pours out a cup, and five streams of wine flow out from it.

Background: In Celtic tradition, the Wall of Knowledge had five streams which flowed from it, each one representing one of the senses by which knowledge is acquired. The ways of the

Grail are many, but each leads to the truth of knowledge.[5]

Meaning: She is intuitive and sympathetic, her compassionate nature embraces all; she imparts the gifts of love to all who encounter her; the depth of her emotion marks her as the upholder of the Grail.

Grail King

Description: Under a mighty oak tree sits the Grail King, holding an earthenware cup. From the tree hangs a golden bowl from golden chains. Near the stream which flows round the tree is a green stone.

Background: When the Grail Knight meets the Grail guardian, he is challenged. Owain encounters such a guardian and throws water upon the green stone nearby which provokes their combat.[30] The golden bowl which hangs from chains is a frequent feature in the Grail legends, and represents the archetypal vessel of quest, by which the world is healed of its divisions.[3]

Meaning: His generosity is proverbial; his creative counselling shows the seeker the way to negotiate the confusions of the quest, for he is the guardian of the hidden mysteries.

Stone: Earth, Winter

Stone Hallow

Description: In the earth of an underground cavern the *gwyddbwyll* board glows with power.

Background: The *gwyddbwyll* (literally, 'wood-cunning') board was one of the prime treasures of the Island of Britain. Whoever possessed it or played upon it was likewise part of the archetypal movements within the land itself.[41]

Meaning: Wisdom; spiritual treasures; consolidation and establishment; attainment; fulfilment; prosperity; the faculty of sensation or instinct; mother-wit.

Stone Two

Description: A river splits into two in a snowy valley. A standing stone is on the left-hand bank.

Background: Palomides, the Saracen knight, having fallen in love with Isolt, spent years in fruitless endeavour to win her from Tristan. He finally became a Christian in her honour, but still failed to win her and chose instead to pursue the Questing Beast.[31]

Meaning: Fluctuation; integrity and scrupulosity cause tardy

stone three

stone Four

beginning to projects; over-prudence; the ability to keep several things in the air; careful choice; instinctive weighing up of values.

Stone Three

Description: A standing stone stands near ploughed fields. On a distant hill is a chalk figure.

Background: The smith was honoured above all men by the Celtic peoples. As well as a craftsman he was often a magician as well.[38]

Meaning: Construction; craftsmanship; professional mastery; practical skills; creative instinct; good organization and skill bring honour and reward.

Stone Four

Description: Beneath a striated hill, a great treasure, including a gaming board, is revealed.

Background: The Thirteen Treasures of Britain are those empowering objects of the land. Whoever holds them is ruler of the land, and hence many of the Hallows descend into modern usage as the regalia of the monarch.[78, 41]

Meaning: Earthly power; conscientious ambition; material

stone Five

stone six

gain; possessiveness; selfishness; spiritual miserliness; time to be generous with others.

Stone Five

Description: In a barren country, a standing stone is seen through a blizzard.

Background: There were times on the quest when the very elements seemed to oppose the seekers. They travelled through lands that were often barren and desolate, by roads long forgotten, where habitations were few and far between.

Meaning: Adversity; insecurity; strain; barren prospects; loneliness; destitution; loss of home or means; the need for a firm instinctive grounding before undertaking a project.

Stone Six

Description: At night, a great fire burns in the middle of a stone circle.

Background: From the time they were built, the stone circles of Britain were symbols of power and might. Apart from their religious significance they were also used for more secular purposes, when poets and story-tellers gathered to continue the great tradition.

Meaning: Material success; good fortune shared; generosity; charity; patronage; gifts; the exchange of matter with spirit; the Great Work.

Stone Seven
Description: A great wall stretching across northern hills. It is broken. Nearby stands a symbol stone.

Background: After his unsuccessful attempt at the quest Lancelot returned to seek again the love of Guinevere. Spurned by her for a time, he went mad, roaming about through the wilderness until he was found and brought back to sanity by Elain of Astolat.[31]

Meaning: Fruitless speculation; anxiety over efforts; lack of fulfilment; fear of failure; the need to live one day at a time and allow events to unfold.

Stone Eight
Description: In a stonemason's yard at sunset, a nearly completed stone carving awaits the mason's chisel.

Background: Before becoming a knight every neophyte underwent a rigorous period of training. Those who went on the Quest, like Perceval, sometimes required additional training before they were fully shaped for their task.[4]

Meaning: Prudence; patient application; discriminating service to a craft; better results through gaining professional skills; apprenticeship; methodical work; detailed preparation.

Stone Nine

Description: In an evergreen clearing stands an ancient stone, marking a place of sanctuary for all wild things, many of whom gather about it.

Background: When Owain sets out on his quest for adventure, he encounters the Wild Herdsman: around him gather all the animals of the forest, for he is their guardian.[30]

Meaning: Accomplishment; enjoyment of solitary pursuits; love of nature; aesthetic pleasure derived from one's goods; relaxation and leisure; ease; fulfilment of physical sensation.

Stone Ten

Description: In a snowy landscape stands a fortress. Two magpies fly with the *gwyddbwyll* board.

Background: The Chessboard Castle is always a place of testing. Those who come there often find a game of chess under way in which the pieces move by themselves.[58]

stone nine

stone ten

Meaning: Tradition; wealth; ancestry; inheritance; property; establishment and permanence; enduring prosperity; the treasures of tradition; ancestral lore.

Stone Maiden

Description: The Stone Maiden walks across the snow bearing the head of man on a platter. Blood falls into the snow. Over a standing stone a raven hovers.

Background: In the early versions of the Grail story, Peredur sees a mysterious procession, in which a maiden bears a man's severed head in a dish of blood. Later on, his quest deepens when he has a vision upon seeing the blood of a duck lying in the snow with a raven feeding from it. [30]

Meaning: She is a wise and discerning student of the mysteries; capable and supremely practical, she listens to the voice of the earth; she is the upholder of the Stone Hallow.

Stone Knight

Description: The Stone Knight rides a brown horse through a mountain pass at sunset. On his arm is the checkered shield.

Background: Bors, Lancelot's brother, is a man with little dynamism, but with a great deal of determination upon the

stone maiden

stone knight

Grail quest. Closest to the average Grail seeker in many ways, he has a deep understanding of human nature.[31]

Meaning: He is a responsible and trustworthy companion; his patient and methodical approach may make him seem rather dull yet he is stubbornly committed to the quest.

Stone Queen
Description: The Stone Queen sits at the window of her castle. Outside, it is snowing. A blackbird perches on her hand. She holds a mirror up to the scene. A *gwyddbwyll* board is set ready for play nearby.

Background: The Queen of the Chessboard Castle is none other than the Goddess of Sovereignty's representative. Her *gwyddbwyll* board is lost by Peredur, who subsequently strives to recover it and win back the Queen's patronage. The board represents the land itself.[30, 41]

Meaning: She is noble and practical; she understands the relationship of all life to the land; she imparts a sense of nurture and security to all who encounter her.

Stone King
Description: The Stone King sits before a trilithon of stone,

with a hound at his feet; on his breast is the checkered emblem of the Stone Hallow.

Background: Bran is the most enduring figure of the inner traditions of the Cauldron and the Grail. A figure of might and power in the early Welsh tales, he is later known as Brons, the Rich Fisherman and brother to Joseph of Arimathea.[45]

Meaning: He is the guardian of traditional lore; by his steady and enduring wisdom, he sustains the land; he teaches patience and responsibility upon the path.

Card Backs

Description: The Goddess of Sovereignty appears on the back of each card, surrounded by the protective rainbow of light, with the four Caers or towers of the Hallow suits and the four Hallows themselves.

Background: Each land has its own tutulary Goddess and its own empowering symbols.

Meaning: When every land of our planet realizes its intrinsic identity, and seeks to manifest its hidden treasures harmoniously, the Goddess of the Earth will once more be empowered and our whole planet protected from those who would do it harm.

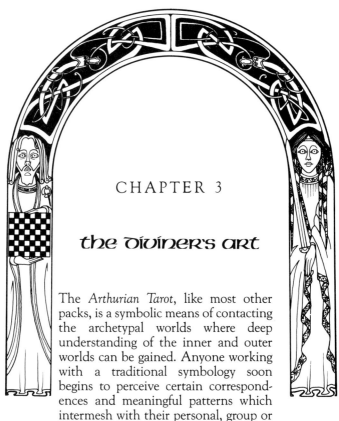

CHAPTER 3

the Diviner's Art

The *Arthurian Tarot*, like most other
packs, is a symbolic means of contacting
the archetypal worlds where deep
understanding of the inner and outer
worlds can be gained. Anyone working
with a traditional symbology soon
begins to perceive certain correspondences and meaningful patterns which
intermesh with their personal, group or
inner life. It is within the potential of anyone to discover these
patterns with the help of a craft such as Tarot divination, so
that one becomes a life-spinner, a pathfinder, a pattern-maker.

No mystical system of divinatory tool can ever replace
personally observed patterns, since these alone are the inner
messengers which convey to us the guidance and sustenance
which we need. However, sometimes a divinatory tool can help
us *trigger recognition* of these patterns. It is only the innately lazy
who rely upon the Tarot as a daily crutch or decision-making
process. Hence the warning in many Tarot books about

over-use of the Tarot for divination.

The primary use of Tarot in divination is that of a symbolic messenger which helps us read the underlying patterns of our life, conveying potent images from the deep inner world of archetypal reality to the everyday world in which we function. The Tarot user's task is to become skilful in this art of interpretation, both personally and for the benefit of others who are unskilled in perceiving their personal life patterns.

You, as Tarot counsellor, must act as a transparent window through which the querent may gaze at the configuration of events and their possible outcome. You are an objective interpreter of the cards, able to elicit the needs and desires of each querent sympathetically and confront them with the blocks which they themselves have set up in the way of those needs and desires. You remain professionally uninvolved in the sense that you personally do not give advice nor take responsibility for someone else's decisions. However, it is important that you give a psychic space for the querent to come to grips with the situation at issue by first creating an atmosphere of trust and relaxed objectivity.

Each card in the *Hallowquest* pack has its own quality which can be borne in mind as you interpret a spread. These qualities may enhance the face meaning which, taken cumulatively, may give a clear overall message to the spread. They can be summarized as follows:

The Greater Powers

These cards represent archetypal or universal energies. When a number of these appear in a spread it indicates that the querent's life is currently governed by inner world direction. It may be that the querent is perfectly aligned with his or her destiny or that the energies ruling this alignment are so strong that they are being brought into play through the querent's life circumstances.

The Lesser Powers

Hallows signify initiating energies. The querent will experience the elemental quality of the Hallowcards which appear in a reading at a deep level; this will manifest perhaps in an unformulated way as a desire to create or bring about an idea in a concrete manner i.e. a painting, a book, a garden or a crêche. A Hallow will often focus a reading quicker than any other card since it frequently gives a key to the querent whose creativity is blocked. The Hallows signify deeply desired change.

The numerical value of the other Minor Arcana cards may also be significant in a spread, especially where two or more cards of the same numerical value appear, i.e. two or more Nines may signify that the querent is currently on the final stages of integrating plans or preparing for the final manifestation of an idea. The reading may indicate how he or she may most effectively bring this about. Individual numbers have the following qualities; as well as indicating the particular path which the querent is travelling:

Twos signify finding direction. The impulse for change which was experienced in the Hallows now makes its first move, sometimes tentatively, sometimes finding reciprocal response as it moves. The impulse to find wisdom.

Threes signify formalization. The idea has received its first impetus at Two but now requires a form or concept to give it shape. The understanding of personal experience derived from the outset of a project.

Fours signify the first attempts to manifest one's idea. Like all try-outs, something positive is always gained in terms of experience, whether the attempt is wholly successful or not. One is administering one's concept and taking responsibility for it for the first time.

Fives signify modification and adjustment. After the first trials of Four, the idea meets problems which have to be solved if the concept is to work effectively. This may seem like a setback, but the necessary adjustment will only come about as a result of facing the obstacles against it.

Sixes signify harmony. After the modification of Five, the idea has found its feet and is a true creation, capable of functioning in all respects. A sense of satisfaction is present.

Sevens signify specialization and extension. It is time to take the idea a step further and experiment with a variety of applications. This sometimes results in an over-extension of energy, but imagination and potential are stretched and the idea will be fully explored for the first time.

Eights signify organization. After the expansive expression of the Sevens, it is time to pull in one's horns and re-assess the situation. This necessary retrenchment is valuable to re-establish one's priorities.

Nines signify integration. With the experience of Seven and Eight behind the idea, it can now be fully integrated. It is at this point that it becomes obvious whether this is the path for you — having seen the idea through all its stages, it must now become part of your life or pass on.

Tens signify culmination. The idea now becomes part of the larger world affecting friends, family and neighbours. The creative impulse of the Hallows is now firmly established on earth as manifest idea-in-action. The world inherits your brainchild which is no longer your responsibility.

Court Cards

Court cards can signify people relating to the querent, aspects of the querent him- or herself, or archetypal messengers of the Hallow court they represent. Their qualities are as follows:

Maidens signify sensation, the way in which you physically perceive things. They are messengers whose advice offers ways out of blocked situations, though this sometimes means taking risks. They open new paths on the Hallowquest.

Knights signify the way in which you intuitively perceive things. They are prime movers who actively demonstrate the strengths and weakneses of their Hallow. They are companions upon the Hallowquest whose help you may call upon.

Queens signify the way in which you feel about things. They are the bearers who channel the energies of their Hallow. They represent stability and dedication to the quest.

Kings signify the way in which you think about things. They are the guardians of their Hallow, giving experience of its wisdom to all who seek it. They represent insight and authority on the Hallowquest.

The Court cards depict the Maidens and Queens as female and the Knights and Kings as male, but these face values do not necessarily denote gender, rather the quality which they bear, i.e. a mystical and idealistic woman who is teaching esoteric wisdom to others might be represented by the Grail Knight, while a practical young man who has just opened a garden centre might be represented by the Stone Queen.

Significators

It has been traditional to draw a card from the pack to indicate the querent at the commencement of a reading. This is normally one of the Court cards; however, there is nothing against drawing one of the Greater Powers instead. If your querent is very self-contained or unwilling to choose a card for him- or herself, then choose one according to your most effective criteria: appearance, emotional feedback from the querent, the nature of problem to be focused upon. If, however, the querent is enthusiastic about the reading process, let him or her shift through the pack until a card is found which seems right.

The *Hallowquest* pack depicts only British racial types because its mythological impetus is from the Arthurian legends. If you or your querent are of another race, do not hesitate to draw whatever card seems most appropriate to you using the *Hallowquest* qualities or the meanings of any card as a guideline for your decision.

Many querents require exact timing from their readings, e.g. 'When will I get married?' 'How long will it be till I get another job?' The Tarot does not seem to be a very accurate device for telling time, but following the example of Gail Fairfield's method[7] it is possible to use the *Hallowquest* pack for this kind of detail.

Swords Spring
Spears Summer
Grails Autumn
Stones Winter

For more precise interpretation, the Greater Powers from Hallow to Queen may be signified in the following way:

Sword
Hallow : 21–27 Mar
Two   : 28 Mar–3 Apr
Three   : 4–10 Apr
Four   : 11–17 Apr
Five   : 18–24 Apr
Six   : 25 Apr–1 May
Seven   : 2–8 May
Eight   : 9–15 May
Nine   : 16–22 May
Ten   : 23–29 May
Maiden : 30 May–5 Jun
Knight : 6–12 Jun
Queen   : 13–19 Jun

Spear
Hallow : 20–26 Jun
Two   : 27 Jun–3 Jul
Three   : 4–10 Jul
Four   : 11–17 Jul
Five   : 18–24 Jul
Six   : 25–31 Jul
Seven   : 1–7 Aug
Eight   : 8–14 Aug
Nine   : 15–21 Aug
Ten   : 22–28 Aug
Maiden : 29 Aug–4 Sep
Knight : 5–11 Sep
Queen   : 12–18 Sep

Grail
Hallow : 19–25 Sep
Two   : 26 Sep–2 Oct
Three   : 3–9 Oct
Four   : 10–16 Oct
Five   : 17–23 Oct
Six   : 24–30 Oct
Seven   : 31 Oct–6 Nov
Eight   : 7–13 Nov
Nine   : 14–20 Nov

Stone
Hallow : 19–25 Dec
Two   : 26 Dec–2 Jan
Three   : 3–9 Jan
Four   : 10–16 Jan
Five   : 17–23 Jan
Six   : 24–30 Jan
Seven   : 31 Jan–6 Feb
Eight   : 7–13 Feb
Nine   : 14–20 Feb

Grail		*Stone*	
Ten	: 21–27 Nov	Ten	: 21–27 Feb
Maiden	: 28 Nov–4 Dec	Maiden	: 28 Feb–6 Mar
Knight	: 5–11 Dec	Knight	: 7–13 Mar
Queen	: 12–18 Dec	Queen	: 14–20 Mar

Using this method it will be seen that each of the Hallow cards (the Aces) fall within the week of the Spring and Autumn Equinoxes and the Summer and Winter Solstices. Leap Year Day, 29 February, always falls within the card of the Stone Maiden. The Kings, if they are drawn using this method, signify the season rather than an exact week. If one of the Greater Powers is drawn, then this signifies that a crucial factor has yet to be determined: either the querent has not resolved the matter to allow the free flow of the problem in hand or else an outside factor is at work. Study the cards drawn carefully for their surface value and meaning.

You have decided to set up in business as a Tarot consultant or counsellor. How do you proceed? Word of mouth is your best advertisement, but you can always advertise locally in order to get your consultancy on the road. Where are your clients going to consult you? If you cannot spare a special consultancy room, then ensure that you have a clearly designated corner of another room especially set aside, uncluttered by your family's belongings. Make it welcoming and comfortable, whether you have cushions on the floor or a good sized table with two chairs. Decide whether your querent is going to sit beside you, so as to be able to see the cards, or facing you.

Your first client arrives, perhaps uncertain or anxious, sceptical or expecting to hear only the worst, distressed or waiting for confirmation of what he or she already knows. Break the ice with tea or coffee and get to know your client a little better. Find out what her expectations are exactly, so that you will know how to pitch your reading. Outline the service you can offer, stressing truthfully that it will be up to the querent to implement what the reading tells her. For the worried or stressed client, ensure that she is aware that the reading is confidential. Allow all querents to feel that they are safe in your consultancy room and that they can consider it a free space in which they are temporarily free from the anxieties which beset them. This is very important, for it frees the querent's mind, enabling it to be receptive to the message of the reading.

Now many clients approach a Tarot reading with the attitude of seeing 'how good you are', meaning that they have come in the spirit of an audience attending a spiritualist meeting or a mind-reading performance. If you are psychic, they will get the message anyway, but if you are not, say so. The most important thing for the tarot counsellor is to know the nature of the problem or issue in question, how the querent feels about it and what they need to know about it. Feedback is essential for the non-psychic, for it helps relate the message to the querent's immediately perceived needs.

It may be that the querent does not really know what question should be asked and here a short general reading 'How things stand at present', may suffice to elicit the querent's response, so that you can both focus on a particular problem. Most people are not constructively introspective or aware of the fears which beset them at a deep level. One short reading will uncover the topsoil sufficiently for the counsellor to delve deeper.

Don't be afraid to write down the querent's question/s; get the querent to do this if she seems to have difficulty focusing her needs. There may be specific questions arising from a central issue, concerning time, involvement, commitment or obstacles. Devise your own spreads to accommodate these questions. In Chapter 4 there are a number of suggested spreads and guidelines for devising your own with the querent's help.

When the question is established, get the querent to shuffle the cards while mentally repeating the question. The cards are the oracle, you are only their interpreter. The shuffling should last as long as seems right for the querent who should then place the cards face down on the table and cut them, if this is your practice. Now lay them out in your chosen spread. During the shuffling and spreading try to discourage the querent from talking, which many will do nervously, thus distracting themselves from the divinatory process.

Now scan the cards, noting how many kinds of Greater or Lesser Powers and their numerical values. Take into account the surface meanings as well as the hidden qualities possessed by each card. Next notice relationships between cards which seem to reinforce the overall message of the reading. Next relate the individual cards to their positions.

Analysis and interpretation is a very personal thing, and you may find that your style of presentation varies considerably between different querents. You will probably want to examine the cards silently before making any comments. If you find it hard to break into the reading then tell the message like a story, making a string or chain or events which grow out of each other. At other times the words will just rise in you, and the overall message will be an obvious one. When the message is unclear to you as the interpreter, it may mean that the querent has not sufficiently focused on the issue at hand. At other times, a reading will seem inconclusive and raise other issues which you may wish to explore using a different sort of spread.

The most important thing is to be flexible. If a card which you have previously filed in your brain as being broadly beneficial in effect appears in a negative position then read it as such, e.g. the Empress appearing in the 'What is hindering you' position would indicate that the querent is spending too much time looking after other people to the detriment of his or her own well-being, or that the querent has allowed him- or herself to get domestically cosy at a time when he or she needs to be more adventurous.

Don't be afraid to state what the cards relate to you, but be sensitive about the way you phrase this to the querent. If you read an accident as a result of careless driving as a possible outcome, then reinforce the message of the cards by advising the querent to improve concentration when driving, or to refrain from driving if tired. Similarly, if an operation or illness seems lurking on the horizon of possibilities, look deeper into the reading to discover the causes of this and whether the querent can improve his or her own health by the avoidance of stress.

Divination is not about doom and gloom, although most of the historical examples we possess, e.g. Julius Caesar's Ides of March warning, the witches' prophecy that Macbeth would never be killed by 'one of woman born' etc. seem to be of this variety. It is true that humanity usually remembers the bad rather than the good news. 'Sufficient unto the day is the evil thereof'. It is not the Tarot consultant's task to add to the burden of life's cares, but to help the querent steer between the reefs and find the most effective way of living by means of the Tarot.

Tarot counselling can be a very rewarding process. You as the reader will be putting clients in touch with the influences of the Otherworld perhaps for the first time. You will be responsible for helping other people to help themselves by pointing out the message of the cards. The querent will draw clues and important keys from your interpretative skills which will empower him or her to focus major life directions. This reciprocal reading process thereby passes beyond the superstitions of fortune-telling into the deeper realms of real divination, where the cards speak directly to the querent bringing their message of guidance and hope.

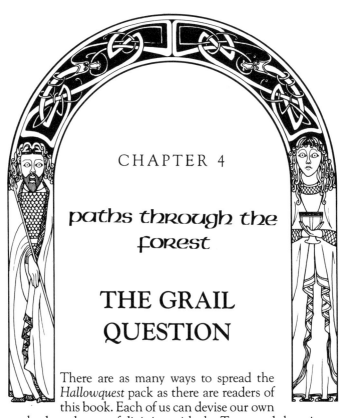

CHAPTER 4

paths through the forest

THE GRAIL QUESTION

There are as many ways to spread the *Hallowquest* pack as there are readers of this book. Each of us can devise our own methods and ways of divining with the Tarot, and there is no necessity to stick to the same spreads over and over, unless you are learning your craft.

Making your own spreads is like finding your own paths through the forest: an adventure in discovery. The time-honoured spreads, like the Celtic Cross and the Zodiac spreads have not been given in this chapter, since there are many books which repeat these time and again. The spreads which follow are suggested uses only: your own spreads are as good as these, if not better, since they will be tailored to suit your needs and those of your querent. Gail Fairfield's book *Choice Centred*

Tarot gives many suggestions on how to formulate your own spreads.[7]

The following spreads come with sample readings, which will give the reader a chance to see how they work in action. The only traditional spread given here is the Tree of Life spread, p.129. Before deciding to read for a querent, the most important thing is to gauge the kind of spread you will need: this will depend very much on the nature of the question to be asked.

You may wish to start the reading with a three-card spread to give the general drift of the consultancy session or to help clarify an unfocused question. You may start with one reading and go on to use another to further define the querent's problem. Tarot consultants are not made of cast iron, however, and two readings a client per session is probably quite enough. Occasionally clients can be very pressing. If they wish to know more, get them to book another appointment.

To help you decide which of the following spreads would be most useful for your purposes, here is a breakdown of their uses:

General clarifying spreads:	*Prydwen's Anchor*
	Tree Of Life
Identifying who you are, the real self:	*Merlin's Mirror*
Escape from self-limitations:	*Mabon's Gate*
Finding your elemental balance:	*Sovereignty's Spread*
Uncovering past karmic responsibility:	*The Excalibur Spread*
Revealing unconscious potential:	*The Three Worlds*

You will undoubtedly discover that these readings will not always fit your needs and you can adapt and reshape them as necessary. Perhaps the most important thing in divination is 'the right question'. Like the Grail question which, when asked, can resolve all problems, the querent's question must be correctly phrased for the diviner's art to have any effect.

Questions like 'Will I marry Jim or Bert?' will just not do, because they are not sufficiently defined. Questions like 'Will

I get a new job?' may be inadequate because other questions have not been posed first, such as, 'What has caused me to be without work?' Much of divination is concerned with self-knowledge and this can only be elicited by questioning. This is hard enough for oneself; eliciting such answers from querents can be uphill work, especially if they have resigned responsibility for themselves into the hands of providence, the state or your Tarot cards!

Your divinatory skills should foster self-responsibility in your querents as well as a healthy degree of incredulity and hard questioning. Our mother-wit or common sense is sadly neglected, no more so than in esoteric areas of life where credulity and resignation of personal responsibility are frequently paramount. The Tarot consultant needs to bear in mind the fact that many people are spiritually impoverished to the point of starvation and that they will seize on any prop to support their life-style, including the Tarot. Therefore, it should be with compassionate insight that the consultant should choose the most appropriate method of questioning the querent.

It is so that the most appropriate spread should be sought, for the ground of divination by Tarot is the questioning spread. The spread demarks part of the querent's spiritual journey, his or her personal quest for meaning and truth. So do not be afraid to abandon your favourite spread if your querent's needs are specific, even if it means you must invent one for that one session.

It is by means of the Grail question that the Wasteland is healed, but until it is asked, nothing can be restored to its full potential.

PRYDWEN'S ANCHOR SPREAD

Many Tarot consultants find that they need a good, general

spread to answer general questions like 'What is happening now?' Such a spread should present the prevailing circum-

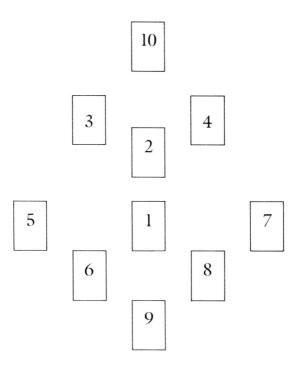

Fig. 4.1: Prydwen's Anchor

stances and surrounding factors in such a way that the querent can clearly see how their present life is configured. Prydwen's Anchor is such a spread and like the anchor on that enduring ship of Arthur's, it shows the factors which give the querent a hold on everyday life.

Meanings of Positions

1. General circumstances prevailing. What is happening now.
2. What is my current direction?
3. How am I preventing the free flow of my life?
4. What opportunities are currently available to me?
5. Home/family factors.
6. Job/vocational factors.
7. Relationship factors.
8. What should I become self-aware of?
9. The past.
10. The future/possible outcome.

Sample Reading of Prydwen's Anchor Spread

Margaret was a teacher with a young family and a husband with whom she was clearly bored. She complained bitterly of his behaviour and the way he had stalled about their impending house-move which had become necessary for the sake of the family space. She needed a general reading just to get her ideas in order. I drew the Spear Queen as her significator, explaining that she was probably more usually a Grail Queen, that the present circumstances made her appear in this guise. She drew the following:

1. The Cauldron
2. Sword Six
3. Guinevere
4. Spear Eight
5. Grail Knight
6. Prydwen
7. Grail Four
8. Spear Four
9. Grail Eight
10. Grail Ten

The reading contained four Grail cards, thus indicating that Margaret's emotional life was at issue here. There were also two

Fours and two Eights, which showed that she was at the difficult time of her life when she had given the first fruits of her talents and was now having to adjust her initial ideas in a more sophisticated way. She had, in fact, got to allow some growth in her life.

The Cauldron showed that she was in need of some serious regenerative energies, that she had recognized the need for harmony in her life and was now seeking the means. The Sword Six showed that she was indeed moving from the old ground she had held into unknown regions. Indeed she was full of the impending move which seemed to dominate her thoughts sleeping and waking. When I suggested that she had let herself become too cosy and domestic and was perhaps blocking the move, she resisted this, but the appearance of Guinevere seemed to bear this out. She was currently surrounded by many possible opportunities to further her move, and she admitted she had been searching the pages of the *Times Literary Supplement* for new teaching posts.

She clearly saw her family in a very idealistic light and had not, unlike some women, succumbed to feelings of guilt on returning to work. She was proud of her children's intelligence and burgeoning abilities and foresaw rosy futures for both of them. Her position at work was a good one and much appreciated, but while she was committed to teaching, she was not attached to her present post. Indeed, the reading gave me the impression she was packed and ready to go at any time. The Grail Four showed that she was not working hard enough at her marriage and that the problems she had experienced with her husband were partially as a result of her own selfish laziness. I could only hint at this, since she strongly resisted any suggestion that she was at fault. The Spear Four showed that she should loosen up and enjoy herself more often, possibly take up her neglected social life which had suffered as a result of her twin roles as teacher and mother. Grail Eight seemed to reinforce Sword Six in that she had been moving away from past endeavours and was preparing to launch herself on the world in a new way for a long time. The future seemed to hold every hope of a more settled family life, especially once they had moved and had more space and time for each other.

Margaret has not been back in touch with us since this reading, but she certainly had the determination to effect her plans, and the resilience of character to help her through the necessary growing period with her husband.

MERLIN'S MIRROR SPREAD

We each of us need to know ourselves better: this is the prime directive of esoteric living and without it we are directionless and unhappy because we can never solve the reason why things do not go right with our lives. Some people spend their whole lives blaming circumstances or other people for their misfortunes, but fail to register their own inadequacies as being at the root of the matter. The Merlin's Mirror Spread reflects our three faces: the one we show to others, the one we would like to be, and the real self which often lies hidden at the centre.

Meanings of Positions

1. The face I show to the world.
2. The reasons why I assume this mask, my hidden fears.
3. What I expect to gain by presenting this persona.
4. What am I doing with my life?
5. Who I would like to be.
6. What is preventing me from becoming this person?
7. What opportunities am I avoiding?
8. How do I envisage my life becoming?
9. The real me.
10. What is my life purpose?

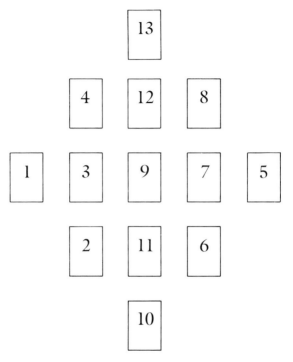

Fig. 4.2: Merlin's Mirror

11. What still needs to be assimilated into the real me?
12. What inessential part of my persona am I shoring up?
13. The next step on my life journey. What I should bear in mind.

Sample Reading of Merlin's Mirror Spread

Alex, a bookshop proprietor whom I knew well, came for a reading. He was middle-aged and rather dour in appearance, but this belied a warm, friendly character. I knew others who thought him cold, and rather steely in his everyday dealings in the shop. He was well acquainted with the Tarot and usually read for himself, but felt that he needed more objective perspectives about him and his life's direction. We discussed the possibilities and chose the Merlin's Mirror spread as the most appropriate for his needs. When I suggested the Sword King for his significator, he laughed but agreed that this was the one. He drew the following cards:

1. Sword Eight	7. Lady of the Lake
2. Stones Eight	8. Round Table
3. Merlin	9. Spear Two
4. Sword Knight	10. Stone Ten
5. Guinevere	11. Grail Knight
6. Spear Three	12. Sword Queen
	13. The White Hart

Looking overall, we noticed that there were five major arcana cards out of a possible 13. This signified a complete change around for Alex as these macrocosmic factors made their appearance in his life. Moreover he had drawn Major Arcanas I, II, and III, which showed that this change would be as the result of a chain of connected causes. Otherwise, the reading seemed fairly well balanced.

The reading began significantly with two Eights, which showed that Alex was in a condition of recapitulation and self-assessment. The face which he showed to the world was a rather depressing one. We joked that this might be good for business! But it appeared that his pessimistic and often complaining mask had come about as the result of anxieties to do with his own industry and application to his business. He was so busy working towards a self-image of high-powered selling, and so anxious about his abilities to keep going, that this reflected itself in the rather crabby exterior he showed to others. This seemed borne out by his life's direction, represented by the Sword Knight, which showed that Alex pursued a single-minded course of ruthless activity, keeping in touch with the book business and furthering his outlets. He felt that this was putting the case too strongly, and that his shop was the basis for more than furthering his financial gain. This indeed seemed the case, from a reading of position 10, which showed him deeply interested in the communication and dissemination of wisdom to all comers.

His idealized self was represented by Guinevere, a figure almost totally the reverse of his persona. He would like to be a reflective and tranquil person, able to enjoy the fertile and creative ideas which emerged from his own reading. The Spear Three showed that he never allowed himself to rest long enough and so enjoy the kind of tranquillity he longed for. He was virtually a workaholic, unable to pass up the offer of new outlets and activities. The opportunity to assimilate some of the books which he sold but never had time to read seemed one of his greatest regrets. If he were ever able to take on the persona of Guinevere in his own life, he would doubtless find a complete change such as he longed for. In fact he admitted he felt he was blocking the flow of new opportunities by running after so many invitations to speak at conferences and attend bookfairs.

He still needed to assimilate the Grail Knight side of himself: the dreamy, idealistic side which only he could give assent to. This was reinforced by the appearance of the Sword Queen, which seemed to suggest that he was unable to delegate some of the mundane tasks at the shop to a capable assistant, keeping himself severely to his allotted tasks. His next step should be dictated by his understanding of the White Hart: he should recognize that he was not wholly self-sufficient and that he could afford to take some risks in order to give his real self time to relax. Position 9 showed that he was a courageous organizer able to make creative decisions, but that this fundamental part of himself wasn't getting a chance. He needed to use the same energies he had been using in his bookselling and apply them to himself, thus opening up forgotten areas of his being.

He is still tending to burn the candle at both ends, but says that he is striving to overcome the temptation to work all day and night as well, by positively 'knocking off' at eight o'clock every night and relaxing with a book. His customers have even been surprised by his unwonted humour, as he is making a genuine effort to lighten up.

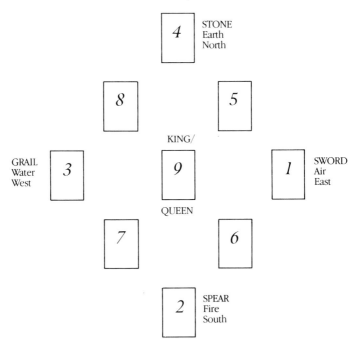

Fig. 4.3: Sovereignty's Spread

SOVEREIGNTY'S SPREAD

We are each potentially the king or queen of our own inner realm of awareness, but we seldom act as though this was so because we really do not know ourselves well enough. Sovereignty's Spread shows how our strengths and weaknesses are configured, using the basic elemental ascriptions of Hallow positions and the four humours. The resultant reading shows us 'the body politic' — ourselves as the realm of Logres, centred at its heart as the king or queen, surrounded by our empowering or disempowering hallows, and subject to crucial decisions which must be based on our perceptive faculties.

Meanings of Positions

1. The Intellectual faculty. Thinking.
2. The Intuitive faculty.
3. The Emotional faculty. Feeling.
4. The Instinctive faculty. Sensation.
5. Fears.
6. Unconsidered, hasty decisions.
7. Hopes.
8. Considered, introspective decisions.
9. Oneself as sovereign.

Sample Reading of Sovereignty's Spread

A young woman named Maura wanted to know just where her life was getting in a mess. After an active career as a fashion designer, she had virtually ceased to do any work, even freelance, after the birth of her two children. She felt frustrated but sensed that she was somehow to blame for her predicament. We chose this spread for her so that she could see for herself the way she had arranged her life according to principles of which she was totally unaware. She drew the following cards:

1. Spear Four   6. Sword Seven

2. The Wounded King
3. Grail Ten
4. Sword Ten
5. Stone Hallow

7. Sword Two
8. Grail Maiden
9. Sword Eight

Interestingly, she chose the Spear Knight as her significator: this was how she still saw herself, though she was the first to agree that this was far from the picture that emerged. A quick scan of the elemental positions showed that she was strongest in the southern Fire quarter, since one of the Greater Powers was there. The reading showed a preponderance of Swords, indicating that she was avoiding coming to grips with the eastern, Air quarter of her kingdom.

At position 1 she showed an avoidance of serious intellectual effort in her life, while at 3 an over-reliance on the emotional cohesion of her family life. Other warning factors showed at positions 4 and 5 where her inability to come to terms with the Stone Hallow, inner wisdom, caused her to be deeply unstable in the practical side of her life. The Wounded King at 2 showed that she was capable of considerable leaps of insight, even at the expense of her own comfort, in order to arrive at a given solution. This had made her a good, even ruthless designer, sacrificing her health in order to succeed.

She had sometimes deprived herself of easy options and allowed others to walk in over her, in order that she might pursue her hunches (Sword Seven). The Sword Two showed that she had so blinkered herself by following her self-chosen course that she was ambivalent about her own prospects. Where she had taken time to consider her own needs, she had brought a great deal of insightful satisfaction (Grail Maiden). But the final card, Sword Eight, showed her totally disempowered, surrounded by a great deal of self-created problems.

Maura was visibly upset at the truth of this reading, and we spent some time going through it and analysing parts of her present life and where she might seriously integrate her best resources, while confronting the worst problems. Her distrust of her instinctive, earthy life seemed at first to be at odds with her decision to have a family and sacrifice her career to their needs; but we discovered that she was courageously attempting to integrate this part of her life, albeit unknowingly, and that her chosen significator was descriptive of her decision. The instinctive faculty, which worked strongest in her inner realm, was in fact over-active and needed to be balanced out by concentration on the Stone Hallow, the element of Earth.

The numerous Swords which overran the spread indicated that she had voluntarily consigned her intellectual abilities into limbo. The fact that she was obviously highly intelligent

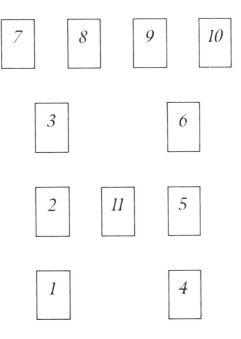

Fig. 4.4: Mabon's Gate

and articulate made me stress how much she must find a suitable outlet for her ideas. She said that she had been toying with the idea of some free-lance work but that her children and various domestic concerns had caused her to put off taking the first step.

I heard from her subsequently that she had taken up a post as tutor at an adult institute for further education, teaching fashion design, for two nights a week. A baby-sitter had been found for these evenings and she was looking forward to returning to full-time work as soon as her children were both attending school.

MABON'S GATE SPREAD

Most of us have ideal situations which exist in our heads but which never come to fruition because we cannot pass through the door which leads beyond our everyday lives. This reading helps clarify the means by which we can both block and help ourselves to achieve our aims, giving a key to unlock that door. The release of Mabon from his long imprisonment was the basis for this spread.

Meanings of Positions

1. What I would like to achieve.
2. What is blocking me from achieving it?
3. How I unconsciously block myself.
4. What I have already achieved.
5. What helped me achieve it?
6. How have I helped myself?
7. The way my idea is received by others.
8. Who will benefit from my idea?
9. How I can revisualize my idea.

10. The next step.
11. The key which will unlock the door to achievement.

Sample Reading of Mabon's Gate Spread

Ian, a young musician, came for a consultation. He was one of those unusually lucky people who had achieved fame quite early in life but was now heading for middle-age and finding that opportunities were not falling into his lap as they once did. He had done no major gigs for quite a while and was wondering when things were going to pick up again. The possibility that he might never again achieve the peak of his early success had not occurred to him and he had spent about the last five years pretending to himself that this was a temporary lull. He was a stubborn and self-willed person who took himself very seriously and had consulted us only at the urging of a mutual friend. As he was quite unfamiliar with Tarot, I chose a significator for him: the Stone Knight.

He drew the following cards:

1. Guinevere
2. Grail Knight
3. Grail Four
4. Sword Queen
5. Sword Five
6. Sword Five
7. The Flowering of Logres
8. Grail Queen
9. The Lady of the Lake
10. Stone Six
11. The Star

It became immediately apparent that Ian was bubbling with creativity from the preponderance of the Grail suit. There were four Major Arcana cards and the reading both began and ended in Major cards. At first glance the reading looked almost too perfect, as though Ian was trying to make a good impression. As a performer, he had been using the rudiments of esoteric skill of course, and knew unconsciously just how to affect an audience.

Ian's prime aim was to continue as a successful performer and musician and so the appearance of Guinevere was no surprise. His current blockage seemed to arise from a profusion of opportunities; he admitted that he accepted several bookings via his agent who had presented them in rosy colours, but they had mostly turned out to be second-rate gigs. This had led in turn to a reluctance to accept any bookings at all in the last few months, which he had spent in prepraring another great performance, but which in reality had been spent in idleness. His excuse for this was that he needed the rest. This seemed to be true from the Grail Four which signified staleness and stagnation.

The Sword Queen's appearance showed that he had in the past achieved a great deal due to someone's incisive and well-planned action. This did not seem to emanate from Ian himself and when questioned, he said that all his earlier work had been organized by an excellent road manager who had the right touch. She had given him a great deal of helpful advice and helped him plan his next tour in the most effective way. The Grail Five suggested that he had been so successful initially due to a series of lucky breaks where tours had been cancelled at the last moment and he had been able to step into the breach at short notice. He reluctantly admitted this when asked but was adamantly against the suggestion of the next card, Sword Five, that he had capitalized on others' misfortunes and continued to do so unconsciously. He so firmly refuted this that I suspected it was indeed the case, but that he could not see this rather sinister side to himself.

The Flowering of Logres showed just how universal his appeal was. Indeed I sensed from the overall reading that it was perhaps a little too appealing and that his 'sound' had blended into the overall rock scene so well that he was no longer quite so distinctive a musician as he had once been. At position 8, the Grail Queen indicated a woman with whom he was involved. He was quite willing to admit to a girl-friend in whom he was quite interested but his air of unconcern seemed to hide a deeper affection and need. Some of his desire to succeed was a need to prove himself to her, I felt.

The Lady of the Lake at position 9 seemed to signify a need to go deeper into the ideas which fuelled his music. I was aware that he was using mythological and sometimes esoteric themes in his lyrics, and this seemed to suggest that he needed to explore them more meditatively and be actively affected by them if his music was to emerge sounding refreshed. His next step was definitely to become a little more generous to other performers in his field; to help them as he had once been inadvertently helped by others. There really seemed to be a karmic message coming through the cards here, relating back to positions 5 and 6. Perhaps by employing some of the new talent in his backing team, he would gain both success and a clear conscience. The key to the door for Ian was The Star of Prophecy — the best possible augury for someone of his ambition. If he was sensitive to the tides of the times, he would indeed make a come-back, with possibly more success than before.

He has since achieved some success by moving into the video business. Two of his backing group have just formed a successful duo which has reached the charts. Ian struck me as a difficult person to like intimately: someone who needed to be loved and to find the well-springs of love within himself. Perhaps that is reflected in Guinevere at the beginning of the reading.

THE EXCALIBUR SPREAD

Sometimes a conventional spread is not sufficient to pin-point the querent's difficulties. They may be too deep-seated, possibly stemming from karmic factors from past lives. The querent may be finding recurrent difficulties, all variations on a theme. If such information crops up either as a result of a reading or in conversation with a client, be very sensitive and listen hard. If the querent states, for example, that people are *always* letting her down, or that she *never* seems to be able to hold down a job, then be suspicious. The 'nevers' and 'always' which occur in conversation denote ingrained problems which are not being faced.

The Excalibur Spread is not suitable for all querents. Not everyone believes in reincarnation, and some who do are so credulous and gullible that it would be a disservice to confront them with such a reading. This spread does not touch in any detail with the previous incarnation/s, but gives a general and overall quality to the kind of person the querent once was and probably still is, since incarnational lessons recur in our present life if we have passed them up in a previous one.

If you feel that the querent may really need regression therapy which can be a powerful and often distressing method of shifting karmic problems into current awareness, then do not attempt to do this yourself unless you are really well qualified. Do not send them to anyone who you suspect is not sufficiently responsible or well-versed in esoteric ethics.

You will probably only use this spread with esoterically-aware clients, in which case, you might conduct the reading in the framework of a simple meditation. Since the sword of Arthur's kingship is guarded by the Lady of the Lake, you might well conduct the querent to a short inner journey to that island, using the card to trigger the imagery if necessary. Let them look into the lake while shuffling the cards. The sword which emerges has a double-sided blade of great sharpness, and its handle has to be gripped decisively.

Meanings of Positions

1. Who I once was.
2. The lessons I learned in that incarnation.
3. The lessons which I failed to learn.
4. Who I am in this incarnation.
5. The things I find easy.
6. The things I find difficult to accept.
7. Recurrent problems.
8. The best method of confronting them.
9. This life's challenging lessons.

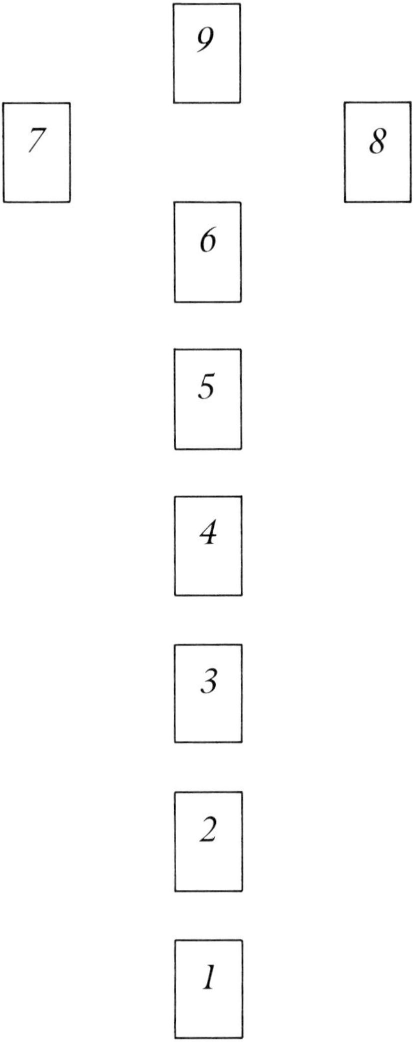

Fig. 4.5: The Excalibur Spread

Sample Reading of
the Excalibur Spread

Josie was a mature student, studying homoeopathy. She hoped
to practice in the next two years, but she was not finding it easy
to get an opening. She had already done several terms' work
helping in a natural health clinic, but the director was not
interested in taking her on. The other places she had worked
were similarly reluctant. Indeed she did seem to emanate
loneliness and unapproachability. She had a string of references attesting to her methodical and devoted work but
these were of little help. She felt defeated and depressed by this
but surprisingly showed no resentment, only resignation.
What was she doing wrong? She seemed honestly bewildered
by this. She was by no means unlikeable, though she was overly
serious and earnest in her speech.

She was interested in esoteric subjects and had a deep
sensitivity to spiritual matters, she said. It turned out that she
had consulted various healers and diviners to help in her
problem, but none of them had anything other than platitudes
for her predicament. I strongly felt that the Excalibur Spread
was right for her and explained it in detail, showing her the
proposed layout. She immediately grew enthusiastic about the
reading, and urged me to give her the cards to shuffle at once.
We did not therefore attempt a meditative reading. She did not
give me time to draw a significator but, interestingly, the card
I would have chosen appeared in the reading anyway.

The cards she chose were:

1. Stone King
2. The Wounded King
3. Grail Ten
4. Grail Maiden
5. Stone Four

6. Spear Two
7. Stone Maiden
8. Arthur
9. The Green Knight

The spread revealed three Greater Power cards, two of which
were located in positions relevant to her present life. There were

also three Stone cards, showing that the problem related to her everyday life and her practical effect on circumstances. At the basis of the reading as the person she had once been was the Stone King, a figure of potent wisdom. I received the psychic impression that this was a figure of some spiritual authority, perhaps an abbot or cardinal, though the feeling I received was definitely monastic. It seemed that Josie had assimilated the lesson of renunciation and self-sacrifice rather too well, if her present life was anything to go by. I questioned her on this point and she obviously was used to living on a very meagre income and making the best of things, although she did not seem to be aware of this. To own a car or her own flat were luxuries beyond consideration, it appeared. She had a small grant paid out of a benefactor's endowment fund, and managed to live on that.

The lesson she had not learned in a previous incarnation, or possibly a set of incarnations, I felt, was that of full integration into family life or into the fellowship of friends. She was the late and only child of elderly parents from whom she felt totally independent, since one had died and the other was in a home. As a result, she did not possess a well-rounded social sense, which made her appear ill-suited for contemporary life.

Her present incarnation found her as a Grail Maiden, very introspective, full of potential enlightenment, but totally unable to express this. Her chosen vocation of healing seemed to me this incarnation's perfect corrective, since the healer's patients become their extended family and they would help her learn much about life's values. She obviously found it easy to study and assimilate facts. Indeed she seemed ridiculously over-qualified for a homoeopath, having a good degree in Classics besides other prestigeous but perhaps superfluous qualifications. This seemed to be the natural residue of previous incarnations in which she had learned these subjects. Her present incarnation did not require her to use these, but her education gave her the opportunity to recapitulate her prior learning. Spear Two showed what she found most difficult in this life was the ability to succeed. It seemed to me that she needed to let things flow more freely and not try so hard, to trust the times and let opportunities come to her naturally, which they certainly would if she could come to grips with the present challenges at hand.

Her recurrent problems were represented by the Stone Maiden — the very card I had mentally decided as her significator but which we had had no opportunity to draw out. I told her this and she was very excited. I also felt that this placement of the card was particularly fortuitous. The Stone Maiden represented her inability to practically apply the wisdom which she had acquired: this is a typical fault of 'spiritual' people and one which she had yet to come to terms with speedily if she was going to make a go of her life. She had made a virtue out of being self-sufficient, but this had not served her well and her lofty humourlessness was taken as selfishness by others.

Arthur represented how she should approach this recurrent problem: by the disciplined use of authority and self-discipline — strengths which past lives had reinforced already but which the monastic role usually plays down. This would enable her to free herself from her somewhat landlocked predicament and bring her into open waters.

It remained only to sum up the present life's lesson. The Green Knight's appearance at this position gave me great hope for Josie although she was somewhat appalled because for her this card normally was represented by The Devil. Her reaction seemed to typify the root of the problem: a fear of facing challenges. The monastic vocation usually absolves the religious from personal decision-making and I challenged Josie on this point. She had indeed taken the line of least resistance throughout her life although her decision to change from an academic to a therapeutic vocation was her personal decision, not forced upon her by either circumstance or at anyone else's behest. This alone showed that she *did* have the ability to overcome her self-limitations and find creative avenues to express her craft.

Josie was obviously greatly empowered by this reading. When

I next saw her, I was on the receiving end of *her* counselling when I attended the natural health clinic. She had had her hair styled and was looking like another person. Gone was the air of loneliness and depression. She was enjoying her new practice thanks to the director whom she had bearded about a possible opening for her at the clinic. Her record of healing was impressive and, after a slightly shaky start, she had gained confidence and insight into her patients' needs. She was, I found, a discerning homoeopath, sensitive in her questioning and deeply perceptive about the cause and effect of illness. When I went to write a cheque to cover the consultancy fee at the end, she refused to accept any money, making me write it for a newly-opened hospice for the terminally ill which was administered by a religious order.

TREE OF LIFE SPREAD

The readings which appear in this chapter have all been aimed at the querent him- or herself and how he or she reacts to the circumstances. This spread has been included to demonstrate how one may appraise a situation, a project or a plan. The Tree of Life is the prime symbolic system of Qabalah, which is a study in itself. For that reason, the spread positions outlined below show the Jewish title of each sephira with its English counterpart. Beneath these are their adapted titles which derive from the qualities and functions of each position.

Meanings of Positions

1. What is the source of the matter?
2. What energy impels it?
3. What form does it take?
4. How is it promoted/assisted?
5. How is it opposed?
6. How is it expressed?

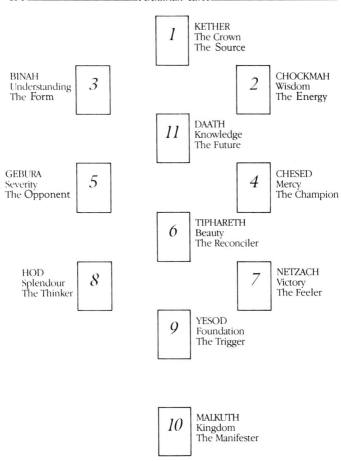

Fig. 4.6: Tree of Life

7. What are your feelings about it?
8. What are your thoughts about it?
9. What triggers its manifestation?

10. How does it manifest?
11. Future prospects.

Sample Reading of Tree of Life Spread

Geoffrey, a young executive, was about to leave his well-paid job to go and work for a new firm. They had offered him huge inducements to leave his position and join them which he felt he couldn't turn down. He knew that the job he was going to was an unknown quantity, since he would be responsible for up-dating his department and bringing it into line with the kind of set-up he had achieved in his last job. His experience and expertise made him highly desirable to his new company, but he did not really know to what extent he had been brought in as a troubleshooter and he was doubtful of certain aspects of the new job. To help distance him from his dilemma, we decided that it would be better to read for the prospects of his new position, rather than for him personally, and how things would turn out. I chose the Sword Knight as his significator. He drew the following:

1. The Cauldron
2. Sovereignty
3. Taliesin
4. Sword Three
5. Grail Eight
6. The Sleeping Lord
7. Prydwen
8. Guinevere
9. Grail Three
10. Stone Four
11. Stone Three

Geoffrey had an amazing six Greater Powers in his reading, showing that this career change was indeed portentious for more than just him personally, it would have far-reaching consequences to his company and those they dealt with. It struck me immediately as a very well-balanced, even strong reading, which reflected Geoffrey's dynamic abilities.

It turned out that Geoffrey wanted to take up his new job because he was partially bored with the old one. He had worked hard to shape the department to its present efficiency but there was little else left for him to do. This seemed reflected by the Cauldron. He was now going to apply his abilities in a new way to a different situation, which was challenge enough for him. He was driven by a deep and overriding integrity in his work, a rarity in the business world, and I wondered with Sovereignty appearing here whether he had ever studied for the bar. He said not, though two of his family were solicitors. The commitment he brought to his work was apparently a byword. He obviously inspired those about him with the same almost religious fervour, if the Taliesin card was anything to go by.

The next two cards caused me a little difficulty since they seemed so contrary to the positions they appeared in: they would have better been swapped over, in my opinion. When I questioned Geoffrey more closely, the picture became clearer. At base, Geoffrey was terrified of separation from that which he loved. His own father had travelled away from home a great deal and had not been a dependable provider to his wife and children. Geoffrey had therefore got on in life as a result of his father's negative example. The Grail Eight suggested that Geoffrey was perhaps passing up opportunities in his old job which might have served him well, and that his new career, while in one way derived from a loss of nerve, sprung from a deep sense of dissatisfaction or failure to achieve all he had planned.

His new career could be signified by the Sleeping Lord, showing the renewal and restructuring of his life. He obviously felt very courageous and self confident about the change, as I saw by the card Prydwen. His thoughts were already creatively engaged in bringing about a harmonious and smooth-running department (Guinevere). A sense of deep satisfaction in turning to a new challenge was the spur to his new career (Grail Three). And he would undoubtedly achieve a great deal of financial success for his new firm, giving his talents to the building up of their assets (Stone Four). The Daath position, which often reveals the unexpected or some hidden feature of the matter, was giving Geoffrey a clear message: despite his hard work for the new company, it might well prove ungrateful in the future and dispense with his services when they had got all that they wanted.

With his youth and prospects before him and a great deal of acumen, Geoffrey decided to make a go of his new career. So far his prospects seem rosy.

THE THREE WORLDS SPREAD

In Celtic mystical cosmology there is a great deal of interchange between the three worlds, as witnessed by the stories of countless heroes and heroines. The three worlds can be roughly defined as follows:

The Underworld — the ancestral place of power, where the roots of creation were laid down. It is not a place of misery and punishment, as in Classical and biblical understanding, but a place of primal power and integration, where skill and empowerment are to be found.

This World — the created, terrestrial world in which ordinary people are born, live and die. It is closely associated with the other two worlds.

The Otherworld — the blessed world of the gods and archetypes, of which mortals had visions, and into which they frequently ventured for enlightenment. It is the burning glass through which eternal light filters into this world.

This spread is particularly valuable for putting people in touch with the hidden alignments of the three worlds, which are still operative for those who perceive them. The Otherworldly level often provides the guiding 'story' which animates the reading.

This spread is quite flexible and does not have a fixed or designated meaning for each card. The three levels are read in order and also in alignment, so that cards 1, 4 and 7 may reveal

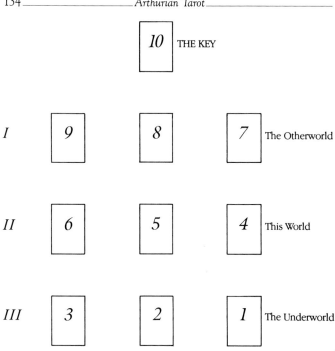

Fig. 4.7: *The Three Worlds Spread*

an interesting or significant factor which the querent is ignorant of or somehow suppressing. The 10th position, the key, gives the keynote of the reading, either expressed as a cumulative factor or else as a way of proceeding.

Sample Reading of the Three Worlds Spread

Valerie was a pleasant and self-possessed woman of about 43. Articulate and expressive, she was somehow tentative and disempowered. She had successfully raised two children who were about to leave home, and was now looking for a job which would fill in her spare time and earn her some money. Her husband was older than she, and was about to retire. She came to me through a mutual friend who consulted me periodically, but she was rather ashamed at resorting to 'fortune-telling', as she saw it, to resolve her difficulties. We talked this through and I put her mind at rest. She was understandably afraid of starting work after so long a time. (She had previously worked for a short while in a shop in the late sixties, but didn't see this as a vocation.) She had explored the possibilities of many jobs, but found that her age and lack of qualifications or experience were drawbacks. I began to feel that I should refer her to a careers guidance officer, who would serve her better, but she insisted she felt I could help her.

I decided that the Three Worlds Spread might help clarify matters, for something seemed deeply buried in her. (The Excalibur Spread would not have been suitable for her, since she was plainly uneasy about esoteric matters.) I let her examine the cards first and did not choose a significator. She exclaimed over some of the landscapes with deep joy and recognition, though she was less happy about some of the other cards. Eventually, she felt confident enough to shuffle the pack and I dealt out the following cards:

1. Stone Five
2. The Spiral Tower
3. Stone Four
4. Sword Queen
5. Grail Hallow
6. Stone Three
7. The Wounded King
8. Stone Maiden
9. Grail Queen
10. Grail King

Although Valerie was dismayed by all the blood in positions 7 and 8 when I turned over the cards, I was very excited at the pattern which stood revealed. At the Underworld level, I noted that a great loss of some kind lay at the basis of Valerie's difficulty, and that this had affected her so radically that her own natural resources had been made unavailable to her. At the level of This World, she appeared as a Sword Queen, ready to swing into action but needing a challenge to empower her.

The Grail lay at the heart of the reading, showing that she was ready to accept a new and fruitful career. Stone 3 showed that she was not afraid of hard work of a rewarding kind. When it came to the archetypal level of the Otherworld, I had to reassure Valerie that the Wounded King did not signify her husband's imminent death, which is what she had assumed. I explained to her about the concept of the Wounded King and the Wasteland, and the way in which the finding of the Grail healed both. She was much cheered when I pointed out that the Grail was at the centre of her reading and operational in her life.

In order to interpret cards 8 and 9 I had to read the spread vertically. The three cards 2, 5, and 8 seemed very significant, since they expressed the very nature of the Grail question. It is the sight of the Grail Maiden bearing a severed head in a dish which is supposed to provoke the Grail question in Peredur, but he fails to ask it. Later on in his story, he sees a raven feasting off a duck in the snow: the combination of the red blood, white snow and black raven provoke him to think deeply on the woman he loves best (she is in fact an aspect of Sovereignty in this story), and he is enabled to get properly started on his quest because he has a purpose at last. I told this story to Valerie and suggested that it might somehow also be hers. She responded very readily by telling me she had indeed suffered a great loss about ten years ago when she lost her third child in a miscarriage and had to have a hysterectomy. She stabbed a finger at the Spiral Tower — 'That's what that's about, isn't it?' she asked. Certainly the very depths of her womanhood had been shaken and she had felt guilty, ashamed and sorrowful all at once.

I then told her about the Celtic tradition of the five streams which ran out of the Well of Knowledge in the Otherworld, depicted in the card of the Grail Queen: that the five streams stood for the five senses by which we regulate our earthly lives. It was our hard work and application which made our lives fruitful (Stone Three), and it was her heritage to drink from this Well of Knowledge herself, for only so would she rediscover the treasures with which she was gifted (Stone Four). She had in fact had the Grail in her hands for a long time but had been unable to drink herself! I went on to the Grail King. I told her that this was her card, for the Grail King was the guardian of this Hallow and her task was to administer the gifts of the Grail to others. By self-questioning and resolution, she would overcome that part of herself which was the Wounded King and heal her psyche of the bitter sorrow of the Wasteland (Stone Five).

I didn't see Valerie again, though I heard from our mutual friend that she had indeed found work as a child minder: her gifts and abilities as a mother were recognized and her lost child had come back to her in a way which seemed the most perfect working out of the Grail story.

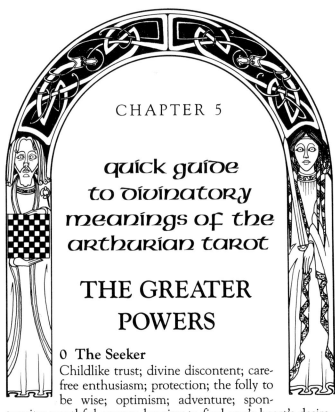

CHAPTER 5

quíck guíde to díoínatory meanings of the arthurían tarot

THE GREATER POWERS

0 The Seeker
Childlike trust; divine discontent; care-free enthusiasm; protection; the folly to be wise; optimism; adventure; spontaneity; youthful energy; longing to find one's heart's desire.

I Merlin
The impulse of creation; imaginative insight; mastery through disciplined skill; initiative; self-confidence; perception on all levels; alignment to and free flow with one's life patterns.

II The Lady of the Lake
Esoteric knowledge; enlightenment; inspiration; wisdom; the ability to impart instruction; counsel; psychic healing; learning.

III Guinevere

Energy in creative growth; material and spiritual wealth; fulfilment; beauty; abundance; fertility; motherhood; health; harmony.

IV Arthur

Leadership; authoritative energy; the wielding of power for the good of all; will-power; organization; courage; responsible love; fatherhood; dynamism.

V Taliesin

Tradition; revelation; inspiration; insight; preservation of heritage; initiation; advice or counsel; transformation of the mundane into the spiritual.

VI The White Hart

Love, both sexual and spiritual; the vision of inner beauty; emotional ties; trust; the marriage of minds and hearts; platonic friendship; fulfilment of desire.

VII Prydwen

Victory; self-confidence; self-discipline; the harnessing of abilities towards a great purpose; tests and trials; achievement; travel; determination; courage.

VIII Gawain

Self-discipline; enduring strength; balanced exercise of one's abilities; health of mind, body and spirit; moral certitude, without self-righteousness; courage to accept challenges; fortitude.

IX The Grail Hermit

Guidance; spiritual truth; illumination; wisdom, counsel – especially from an older or wiser person; introspection; a necessary space for reassessment; inner companionship; maturity; the voice of conscience or one's guardian angel/spirit.

X The Round Table
Evolution; cyclic change; sequential patterns which result from any action; adaptation; incarnation or manifestation of a project; the passing of a concept, project or relationship to another phase; cosmic law or karma.

XI Sovereignty
Justice; equity; rightful rule; vindication of integrity; perception of motives; fair exchange; honest relationships; good measure; balanced reaction.

XII The Wounded King
Wisdom gained through hardship and experience; spiritual insight; commitment to inner principles; the pain and misunderstanding caused by this commitment to others not so dedicated; metanoia — a changing of one's life; inner healing; meditation; purification; the stripping away of inessentials; self-sacrifice.

XIII The Washer at the Ford
The elimination of outworn ideas, stale relationships and static customs; fallowness; sexual union; ecstasy; the disruption of old patterns; renewal; ruthless yet compassionate action.

XIV The Cauldron
Regeneration; fusion; recombination of resources or potentials; tempering outer circumstance by inner values; blending or merging with a new idea; polarized living; correct balancing of one's personality.

XV The Green Knight
Challenge; obstacles which must be overcome; ignorance; self-limitation; inflexibility; unconscious fears realized; stagnation; incisive change; creative possibilities.

XVI The Spiral Tower
Reversal of energies; withdrawal of old customs, phases and

concepts; shocking change; liberation from outworn concepts; humility; the realization of limitations; natural forces at work; a curative illness, e.g. one which expels poisons from the body; loss of cosy security; transfiguration; self-awareness.

XVII The Star
Hope; renewal; the beginning of a new cycle; inspiration; faith born of desire and trust; love of another's good; refreshment; the raising of popular consciousness.

XVIII The Moon
Clear visualization; generation; cyclic patterns of growth; fertility and increase; fluctuation; dreams and visions; introspection; necessary preparation; fallowness; the seasonal round; the tides of time.

XIX The Sun
Innocence; purity; enthusiasm; warmth; a loving heart; joy; freedom; enlightenment; wholeness; health; intolerance of shadows in any aspect of life; clarity; directness; true vocation realized.

XX The Sleeping Lord
Renewal; resurrection; recapitulation of events or ideas; prophetic vision; ending or beginning; forgiveness; adjustment; recovery of that which has been lost sight of; impulse to change one's life.

XXI The Flowering of Logres
Restoration; culmination; triumph; attainment; perfection; rapture; spiritual healing; creative growth; the new aeon.

THE LESSER POWERS

Sword: Air, Spring

Sword Hallow
Incisive energy; the dispelling of illusions; conquest; cham-

pionship; strength and power; love of truth and justice; the power of the mind; rational deduction or perception; light in dark places.

Sword Two
Amnesty or temporary peace; indecision; compromise; suspension of deeply-held beliefs or opinions; hesitation; analysis of the situation is required before action.

Sword Three
Sorrow; separation; deep disappointment; loss; the possession of the thoughts by jealousy; brooding upon personal slights; it is necessary to analyse one's receptivity to the tide of events and acknowledge one's responsibility for others' pain.

Sword Four
Respite; hermetic seclusion; meditation; self-exile or retreat; convalescence; rest; replenishment of spirit; solitude; it is time to reassess one's power and limitations in quiet seclusion.

Sword Five
Defeat; slander; cowardice; unethical behaviour; divisive means; thwarted plans; sloppy or malicious thinking causes things to go awry.

Sword Six
Success after trouble; safety and protection; a journey; new perspectives; difficulties and blockages are cleared as a result of perceptive thought.

Sword Seven
Unstable effort; little progress; plans fail as a result of confused thinking; self-deceit; passivity; over-defensiveness; the need for proper conceptualization.

Sword Eight
Restriction; one's bounden duty; fear of what others say;

bigoted opinions; intolerance; imprisonment; illness; thinking is in bondage; the time for out-worn thought patterns is over.

Sword Nine
Suffering; grave doubts; guilt; premonitions and nightmares; cruelty; despair; depression; inability to take personal responsibility for one's path; the need for a disciplined life-style and commitment to logical thought.

Sword Ten
Life and death decision; the final solution dictated by ruthless logic; pain; affliction; total oppression; masochism; the need for extreme daring and resolution; the acknowledgement and confrontation of karmic debts.

Sword Maiden
She quickly grasps ideas and materializes them; perceptive and discerning, she is vigilant in the cause of truth and justice; she cuts through difficulties by taking the way of self-sacrifice.

Sword Knight
He is incisive and fearless, prompt to defend the weak and swift to halt injustice; he asserts the ideas of right with skill and courage; he is the upholder of the Sword of Light.

Sword Queen
She is intelligent and self-reliant, speaking her mind and not suffering fools gladly; as the defender of the unprotected, she is assiduous and fair-minded; she imparts a sense of justice to all who encounter her.

Sword King
He is the giver of justice, a wise counsellor whose analytical judgements cut right to the heart of the matter; his severity is tempered by impartiality and he shows how self-analysis and love of truth may govern one's life.

Spear: Fire, Summer

Spear Hallow
Creativity; the beginning of a project; innovation; purpose; birth; the faculty of intuition; inspiration; energy; challenge; the healing of all that is corrupt.

Spear Two
Choice; control; mastery; the skilled organization of resources leads to achievement of desire; intuitive synthesis; dynamic drive.

Spear Three
Established strength; controlled intention; intuitive understanding gives an expansive outlook and resulting opportunities; scrupulous responsibility; enterprising initiative.

Spear Four
Completion of an enterprise; a time of festival and celebration; enjoyment of the fruits of one's labours; harmonious conclusion; acknowledgement of intuitive strength.

Spear Five
Contention and strife; salutary struggle; competitiveness; dictatorial attitudes cause obstruction; the need to distinguish between rightful intuition and unassuaged desires.

Spear Six
Victory; advancement realized through steady growth; pride in achievement; recognition; intuitively self-confident; ceremonial honours.

Spear Seven
Courageous ability; success despite opposition; tenacity and persistence upheld by strong intuition; defence of strongly-held beliefs.

Spear Eight

Swiftness; expediency; hasty perpetration of intuitions; prophetic insight; speedy progress and rapid growth; communication.

Spear Nine

Enduring strength; great reserves; dedication to intuitive purpose; obstinacy; defensiveness; the wisdom to prepare against adversity.

Spear Ten

Responsibility; excessive burdens; over-expansion of resources; resolution by test of fire; crisis brings restoration; the need to delegate to others or the readjustment of power in order that the intuitive faculties can operate.

Spear Maiden

She is a resourceful and enthusiastic messenger, faithful and loyal, if uninhibited and forthright; she shows the way through impossible situations by her daring, often by disguise or shape-shifting.

Spear Knight

He is an energetic and impetuous champion; his inspired companionship leads into exciting adventures; but he is fearless of the unknown and his hasty decisions are often risky.

Spear Queen

She is deeply attuned to the needs of the land and has suffered in its service; her grief is well hidden and she is generous and friendly to all; she imparts a deep commitment to the healing of the earth.

Spear King

He is honest and passionate, committed to his intuitive understanding of the land, even to the point of sacrifice; he teaches the ways of healing by his wisdom; he is the upholder of the Spear which both heals and wounds.

Grail: Water, Autumn

Grail Hallow
Fertility; abundance; nurture; spiritual joy; healing; gladness; the emotional faculty; restoration after barrenness.

Grail Two
Love; harmony; partnership; co-operation; concord; emotional reciprocation.

Grail Three
Abundance; solace; fulfilment; fortunate conclusion; the power to communicate joy and gladness; generosity of spirit.

Grail Four
Dissatisfaction; lethargy; accidie; stagnation of the spirit; boredom; the need to establish emotional maturity.

Grail Five
Disillusion; disappointment; vain regret; the ability to learn from mistakes and assess one's limitations; broken agreements or promises.

Grail Six
Rediscovery of one's roots; ancestral memories; the pleasure of remembered links; a sense of tradition and continuance; atavism; karmic recall.

Grail Seven
Self-deception; illusion; an over-active imagination; unrealistic fantasies; the glamour of esoteric practices; the need for emotional discipline.

Grail Eight
Discontinuance of plans; withdrawal of energies and desire; self-pity; movement away from old beliefs and values; an over-

fearful heart; the need to evaluate things from a more universal standpoint.

Grail Nine
Satisfaction; one's heart's desire; security; physical pleasure; emotional contentment.

Grail Ten
Wholeness; perfection of contentment; fellowship and family; the holiness of the home; peace and happiness; the completion of desire shared by others.

Grail Maiden
She is tender and willing; imaginative and loving, she shows the way to fulfil the deepest desires, often through dreams and visions; she exemplifies the way of service.

Grail Knight
He is a meditative and poetic champion, often unconventional; his fertile dreams invite fellow travellers to unexplored regions of the quest; he is incorruptible and dedicated.

Grail Queen
She is intuitive and sympathetic, her compassionate nature embraces all; she imparts the gifts of love to all who encounter her; the depth of her emotion marks her as the upholder of the Grail.

Grail King
His generosity is proverbial; his creative counselling shows the seeker the way to negotiate the confusions of the quest, for he is the guardian of the hidden mysteries.

Stone: Earth, Winter

Stone Hallow
Wisdom; spiritual treasures; consolidation and establishment;

attainment; fulfilment; prosperity; the faculty of sensation or instinct; mother-wit.

Stone Two
Fluctuation; integrity and scrupulosity cause tardy beginning to projects; over-prudence; the ability to keep several things in the air; careful choice; instinctive weighing up of values.

Stone Three
Construction; craftsmanship; professional mastery; practical skills; creative instinct; good organization and skill bring honour and reward.

Stone Four
Earthly power; conscientious ambition; material gain; possessiveness; selfishness; spiritual miserliness; time to be generous with others.

Stone Five
Adversity; insecurity; strain; barren prospects; loneliness; destitution; loss of home or means; the need for a firm instinctive grounding before undertaking a project.

Stone Six
Material success; good fortune shared; generosity; charity; patronage; gifts; the exchange of matter with spirit; the Great Work.

Stone Seven
Fruitless speculation; anxiety over efforts; lack of fulfilment; fear of failure; the need to live one day at a time and allow events to unfold.

Stone Eight
Prudence; patient application; discriminating service to a craft; better results through gaining professional skills; apprenticeship; methodical work; detailed preparation.

Stone Nine

Accomplishment; enjoyment of solitary pursuits; love of nature; aesthetic pleasure derived from one's goods; relaxation and leisure; ease; fulfilment of physical sensation.

Stone Ten

Tradition; wealth; ancestry; inheritance; property; establishment and permanence; enduring prosperity; the treasures of tradition; ancestral lore.

Stone Maiden

She is a wise and discerning student of the mysteries; capable and supremely practical, she listens to the voice of the earth; she is the upholder of the Stone Hallow.

Stone Knight

He is a responsible and trustworthy companion; his patient and methodical approach may make him seem rather dull yet he is stubbornly committed to the quest.

Stone Queen

She is noble and practical; she understands the relationship of all life to the land; she imparts a sense of nurture and security to all who encounter her.

Stone King

He is the guardian of traditional lore; by his steady and enduring wisdom, he sustains the land; he teaches patience and responsibility upon the path.

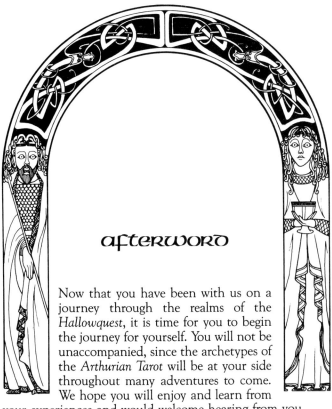

afterword

Now that you have been with us on a
journey through the realms of the
Hallowquest, it is time for you to begin
the journey for yourself. You will not be
unaccompanied, since the archetypes of
the *Arthurian Tarot* will be at your side
throughout many adventures to come.
We hope you will enjoy and learn from
your experiences and would welcome hearing from you.

A *Hallowquest* course is in preparation through which you
may wish to pursue the path begun in this book. A tape
containing some of the meditations in this book will also be
available. Write to us at the address below, sending two first-
class stamps (for readers in the British Isles) or two inter-
national reply-paid coupons (for overseas readers), and we will
keep you informed of future developments, as well as other
related courses in the Arthurian, Native and Goddess
traditions.

BCM — Hallowquest
London WC1N 3XX

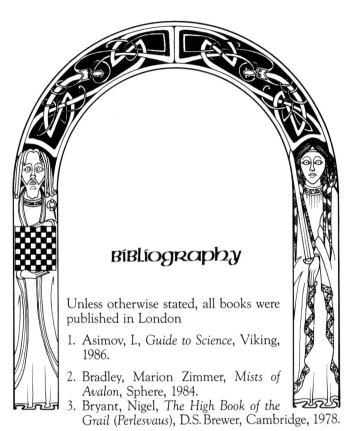

BiBLiOGRAphy

Unless otherwise stated, all books were published in London

1. Asimov, I., *Guide to Science*, Viking, 1986.

2. Bradley, Marion Zimmer, *Mists of Avalon*, Sphere, 1984.

3. Bryant, Nigel, *The High Book of the Grail (Perlesvaus)*, D.S. Brewer, Cambridge, 1978.

4. Chrétien de Troyes, *Arthurian Romances*, trans. D.D.R. Owen, Dent, 1987.

5. Cross, T.P. and Slover, C.H., *Ancient Irish Tales*, Figgis, Dublin, 1936.

6. Curtin, Jeremiah, *Hero Tales of Ireland*, Macmillan, 1894.

7. Fairfield, Gail, *Choice Centred Tarot*, Newcastle Publishing Co., Hollywood, 1984.

8. Geoffrey of Monmouth, *History of the Kings of Britain*, Penguin, Harmondsworth, 1966.

9. ——, *Vita Merlini*, ed. and trans. J.J. Parry, Univ. of Illinois Press, Illinois, 1925.

10. Gilchrist, Cherry, *Circle of Nine*, Dryad Press, 1988.

11. ——, *Divination*, Dryad Press, 1987.

12. Gray, W.G., *Magical Ritual Methods*, Helios Books, Toddington, 1971.

13. Greer, Mary K., *Tarot Constellations*, Newcastle Publishing Co., Hollywood, 1988.

14. ——, *Tarot for Yourself*, Newcastle Publishing Co., Hollywood, 1984.

15. ——, *Tarot Mirrors*, Newcastle Publishing Co., Hollywood, 1989.

16. Gregory, Lady, *Voyages of Brendan the Navigator and Tales of the Irish Saints*, Colin Smythe, Garrard's Cross, 1973.

17. Guss, David M., *The Language of the Birds*, North Point Press, San Francisco, 1985.

18. Hall, L.B., *Knightly Tales of Sir Gawaine*, Nelson Hall, Chicago, 1976.

19. Harf-Lancner, L., *Les Fées au Moyen Age*, Librairie Honoré Champion, Paris, 1984.

20. Hashrouck, M. B., *Tarot and Astrology: the Pursuit of Destiny*, Aquarian Press, Wellingborough, 1986.

21. Karr, Phyllis Ann, *The King Arthur Companion*, Chaosium Inc., Albany, 1983.

22. Kitteridge, G.L., *A Study of Gawaine and the Green Knight*, Peter Smith, Gloucester, Mass., 1960.

23. Knight, Gareth, *The Secret Tradition in Arthurian Legend*, Aquarian Press, Wellingborough, 1983.

24. Korrel, Peter, *An Arthurian Triangle*, E.J. Brill, Leiden, 1984.

25. Lacy, Norris J., ed., *The Arthurian Encyclopedia*, Garland Publishing, Inc., New York, 1986.

26. Lacy, Norris J., and Ashe, Geoffrey, eds., *The Arthurian Handbook*, Garland Publishing Inc., New York, 1988.

27. Loomis, R.S., *Arthurian Tradition and Chrétien de Troyes*, Columbia Univ. Press, New York, 1949.

28. ——, *Celtic Myth and Arthurian Legend*, Haskell House Pubns., New York, 1967.
29. ——, *Wales and Arthurian Legend*, Folcroft Editions, 1977.

30. *Mabinogion*, ed. Lady Charlotte Guest, Ballantyne Press, 1910.
31. Malory, Sir Thomas, *Le Morte d'Arthur*, University Books, New York, 1961.
32. Maltwood, K.E., *The Enchantments of Britain*, James Clark & Co., Cambridge, 1982.
33. Markale, Jean, *Le Graal*, Retz, Paris, 1982.
34. ——, *King Arthur, King of Kings*, Gordon Cremonesi, 1977.
35. Mason, Herbert, *Gilgamesh*, Houghton Mifflin, Boston, 1971.
36. Matarasso, P.M., *The Quest of the Holy Grail*, Penguin, Harmondsworth, 1969.
37. Matthews, Caitlín and John, *The Western Way vol I: The Native Tradition*, Arkana, 1985.
38. ——, *The Western Way vol II: The Hermetic Tradition*, Arkana, 1986.
39. Matthews, Caitlín and Jones, Prudence, *Voices From the Circle*, Aquarian Press, Wellingborough, 1990.
40. Matthews, Caitlín and Pollack, Rachel, eds., *Tarot Tales*, Century, 1989.
41. Matthews, Caitlín, *Arthur and the Sovereignty of Britain: King & Goddess in the Mabinogion*, Arkana, 1989.
42. ——, *The Elements of Celtic Tradition*, Element Books, Shaftesbury, 1989.
43. ——, *The Elements of the Goddess*, Element Books, Shaftesbury, 1989.
44. ——, *Mabon and the Mysteries of Britain: An Exploration of the Mabinogion*, Arkana, 1987.
45. Matthews, John and Green, Marian, *The Grail Seeker's Companion*, Aquarian Press, Wellingborough, 1986.
46. Matthews, John and Stewart, Bob, *Warriors of Arthur*, Blandford Press, Poole, 1987.
47. Matthews, John, ed., *The Arthurian Reader*, Aquarian

Press, Wellingborough, 1988.

48. ——, *At the Table of the Grail*, Arkana, 1987.

49. Matthews, John, *The Elements of the Arthurian Tradition*, Element Books, Shaftesbury, 1989.

50. ——, *The Elements of the Grail Tradition*, Element Books, Shaftesbury, 1990.

51. ——, *Gawain, Knight of the Goddess*, Aquarian Press, Wellingborough, 1990.

52. ——, *The Grail: Quest for the Eternal*, Thames & Hudson, 1981.

53. Nennius, *British History and Welsh Annals*, ed. and trans. J. Morris, Phillimore, Chichester, 1980.

54. Parry, Idris, *Animals of Silence*, Oxford Univ. Press, Oxford, 1972.

55. Racoczi, Basil I., *The Painted Caravan*, L.J.C. Boucher, The Hague, 1954.

56. Raine, Kathleen, *Yeats the Initiate*, Dolmen Press, Portlaoise, 1986.

57. Ross, Anne, *Pagan Celtic Britain*, Routledge & Kegan Paul, 1967.

58. Skeels, D., *Romance of Perceval in Prose, (Didot Perceval)*, Univ. of Washington Press, Seattle, 1966.

59. Skene, William F., *The Four Ancient Books of Wales*, Edmonston & Douglas, Edinburgh, 1868.

60. Spence, Lewis, *The Mysteries of Britain*, Aquarian Press, Wellingborough, 1970.

61. Spenser, Edmund, *The Faerie Queen*, Oxford Standard Authors, New York, 1963.

62. Stafford, Greg, *Pendragon Game*, Chaosium, Inc., Albany, 1985.

63. Stewart, Bob and Matthews, John, *Legendary Britain: An Illustrated Journey*, Blandford Press, Poole, 1989.

64. Stewart, Mary, *The Crystal Cave*, Hodder & Stoughton, 1970.

65. ——, *The Hollow Hills*, Hodder & Stoughton, 1973.

66. ——, *The Last Enchantment*, Hodder & Stoughton, 1979.
67. Stewart, R.J., *Advanced Magical Arts*, Element Books, Shaftesbury, 1988.
68. ——, *The Elements of Creation Mythology*, Element Books, Shaftesbury, 1989.
69. ——, *Living Magical Arts*, Blandford Press, Poole, 1987.
70. ——, *The Merlin Tarot* (illustrated by Miranda Gray), Aquarian Press, Wellingborough, 1988.
71. ——, *The Underworld Initiation*, Aquarian Press, Wellingborough, 1985.
72. Sutcliff, Rosemary, *Sword at Sunset*, Hodder & Stoughton, 1963.

73. Tatz, M. and Kent, Jody, *The Tibetan Game of Liberation*, Rider, 1978.
74. Tennyson, Alfred, Lord, *Idylls of the King*, Penguin, Harmondsworth, 1983.
75. Tomberg, Valentine (Anonymously), *Meditations on the Tarot*, Amity House, Amity, 1985.
76. Treece, Henry, *The Great Captains*, Bodley Head, 1956.
77. Trevelyan, George and Marchatt, Edward, *Twelve Seats at the Round Table*, Neville Spearman, Jersey, 1976.
78. *Trioedd Ynys Prydein*, trans. Rachel Bromwich, University of Wales Press, Cardiff, 1961.

79. Von Eschenbach, Wolfram, *Parzival*, trans. A.T. Hatto, Penguin, Harmondsworth, 1980.
80. Von Zatzikhovan, Ulrich, *Lanzelet*, ed. and trans. K.T.G. Webster, Columbia Univ. Press, New York, 1951.

81. Wang, Robert, *The Qabalistic Tarot*, Weiser, York Beach, Maine, 1983.
82. Webster, K.G.T., *Guinevere: a story of her abductions*, Turtle Press, Milton, Mass., 1951.
83. Weston, Jessie, *From Ritual to Romance*, Doubleday, New York, 1957.
84. White, T.H., *The Once and Future King*, Collins, 1952.
85. Williams, Charles, *The Greater Trumps*, William B.

Eerdman's Pub. Co., Grand Rapids, 1978.
86. Willis, Tony, *Magick and the Tarot*, Aquarian Press, Wellingborough, 1988.

87. Yeats, W.B., *Mythologies*, Collier Books, New York, 1958.

OTHER BOOKS BY CAITLÍN AND JOHN MATTHEWS

Caitlín Matthews

Sophia, Goddess of Wisdom: From Black Goddess to World Soul, Unwin Hyman, 1990.
Voices of the Goddess: A Chorus of Sibyls, Aquarian Press, 1990.

John Matthews

Boadicea: Warrior Queen of the Celts, Firebird Books, 1988.
Celtic Battle Heroes (with Bob Stewart), Firebird Books, 1988.
A Celtic Reader, Aquarian Press, 1991.
El Cid: Champion of Spain, Firebird Books, 1988.
Fionn mac Cumhail: Champion of Ireland, Firebird Books, 1988.
Household of the Grail, Aquarian Press, 1990.
Legendary London (with Chesca Potter), Aquarian Press, 1990.
Richard Lionheart: The Crusader King, Firebird Books, 1988.
Taliesin: the Shamanic Mysteries of Britain and Ireland (with additional material by Caitlín Matthews), Unwin Hyman, 1990.
Warriors of Christendom (with Bob Stewart), Firebird Books, 1988.

Caitlín and John Matthews

The Aquarian Guide to British & Irish Mythology, Aquarian Press, 1988.

The Arthurian Book of Days, Sidgewick & Jackson, 1990.

The Grail Seeker's Companion (audio cassette), Talisman Tapes, PO Box 42, Bath, Avon BA1 1QN.

Walking the Western Way (audio cassette), Sulis Music & Tapes, BCM 3721, London WC1N 3XX.

Also available by the same authors . . .

HALLOWQUEST

Tarot Magic and the Arthurian Mysteries

Hallowquest takes you deeply into the realm of King Arthur. Drawing on the rich mythology of the Celtic-Arthurian legends, Caitlín and John Matthews unlock the subtle levels of the Arthurian Mysteries by means of Tarot magic.

This complete companion volume to the exceptional *Arthurian Tarot* describes the Celtic derivation of the Arthurian legends and their correspondences with early medieval stories, giving the reader a firm traditional foundation to work from. The four empowering Hallows of the Sword, Spear, Grail and Stone appear in the four Tarot suits and form the basis of a modern Grail Quest.

You will meet the gods and symbolic forms which underlie King Arthur's magical realm, as well as encountering the kings, queens, knights and maidens of each of the four castles which stand as elemental guardians of the Arthurian realms. In the course of the many practical rituals, meditations and shamanic journeys included within this book, you will become acquainted with your own inner landscape.

Hallowquest presents a complete initiatory system into the Arthurian Mysteries as well as providing new ways of using the Tarot, including story-telling, ritual and shamanic exploration.